Letters I'll Never Send:
Inspiration

Letters I'll Never Send: Inspiration

SBN-10: 0-98383-831-3
ISBN-13: 978-0-9838383-1-9
Printed in the United States of America.
First printing August, 2011

Introduction

Dear Readers,

The origin of the website, LettersIllNeverSend.com, began with a simple statement, 'You call THAT a break-up letter?!?'

Back in January of 2010, my sister, recently broken up with her fiancé of 12 years, decided to write her letter. You know the one; the letter that finally lets your ex have the Truth - no holds barred. Finally you are able to tell the Truth which has so long been imprisoned in the deepest recesses of your soul. Throughout your relationship, your Truth, tethered by the fear of losing your partner, watched bitterly as the dinner party ended with your Partner drinking too much wine, leaving you once again the designated driver. Your Truth screamed a muffled, "Foul!" as your Partner flamboyantly flirted with strangers. Your Truth balled its fists and pummeled the air as your Partner ignored your text message pleas for communication. All those moments of anger and disappointment, jealousy and betrayal were stuffed down deep, one on top of the other until your Truth finally squeezed through the bars of the dank cell where it had festered. Freed, your Truth rises to the surface to finally be heard! Your Truth wants to sit your ex down, look them straight in the eye, and recount every relationship violation until your ex FEELS the betrayal, LIVES the misery and REGRETS the choices they made until the day they die.

And THIS is usually the ideal time to pick up the pen (or keyboard, as the case may be). For as awesome, powerful and righteous as your Truth is, sometimes trying to get that satisfaction from your ex can leave you damaged from the experience and sometimes opening up your precious and vulnerable heart to someone who hurt you is something that they just don't deserve to see.

That is where LettersIllNeverSend.com comes in. The site offers the outlet for your Truth to be heard, acknowledged, and applauded. In the process of writing it out, you heal. In the process of allowing others to read your Truth, you enable them to heal.

LettersIllNeverSend.com began with a break-up letter but has evolved to encompass every type of letter: the most passionate of love, the darkest side of hate, extreme anger, incredible happiness, deep sadness, heartbreaking grief, profound gratitude, bitter jealousy, and my favorite, tremendous hope.

Hope is the subject that I have chosen as the first book of the LettersIllNeverSend.com series because Hope is the foundation of happiness. These extraordinary letters are written by ordinary people. Some of the letters are directed to a loved one, sometimes they are written to themselves and many times they are written especially for you, the person reading this right now. In reading through these letters, I am inspired by the insight of everyday people. I am inspired to do better, be better, feel better, and live better. Most of all I am inspired to share their insights with you.

In reading this book please understand that although I correct spelling and grammar where necessary, I try to leave the letter 'original' as the reader intended. I can guarantee that you will find grammar errors, typos, etc...but I ask you to momentarily put down the correction pencil so that you can allow yourself to enjoy the message.

My heartfelt thanks go to all the writers who have written words of inspiration on this site. You have certainly touched my life.

Here is to speaking your Truth and finding Hope.

- Admin

Contents

My inspiration:
To Carina, Will, Mom, Paris, Isabel and my family and friends.
Without your love and support these pages would be empty...as would my heart.

A
LETTER
TO
ME

I choose hope.

Those who don't learn from history are doomed to repeat it... That's the old adage the runs through my head when I try and fix the same problem.

But what if this one time it'll work? What if this time it's the right solution?

I don't want you to look at me with an "I told you so." face. I want you to realize that some change can be good. Some ideas can flourish. But you have to let them fail a bit first to find their footing.

I'm putting good thoughts out for a positive result. I'm choosing hope instead of cynicism.

Ready, set, go.

In the Now.

Why is it such a struggle to be happy? We are born with happiness. Sure, we cry when we're hungry, or need attention, or need to be changed...but from the mother's womb we are innately happy beings.
The most fascinating concept for me is that we choose to be miserable. At first I was going to say "choose to be happy"...but that isn't it. If we are innately happy creatures then we would most certainly choose to be miserable. It is an effort to be happy, granted, when there are so many miserable things surrounding us but that doesn't mean we need to be unhappy.

There have been so many days with I have sat in sunny weather and good health wallowing in my own pity. Or I have been anxiety ridden with the happiness I felt because if things are "too good" surely the other shoe will drop.

Just as an infant does not understand the concept of time, so does happiness. The infant is completely in the "now" and cries with hunger, not knowing that food is on its way; cries with fear, not knowing that mama is around the corner; cries with discomfort, not knowing that a clean, diaper and soft powder is minutes from application. The happiness in us can be felt if we simply are in the "now". This, of course, does not apply if you are experiencing a devastating loss...since grieving is a necessary process of healing.
However, the process of being in the "now" allows us to focus on the growing children in front of us, the health that we have (because even if you are suffering an illness, you are alive), the air that fills our lungs, the inside, the outside, the love...

This is a reminder to ME...that I need to be in the now. I need to breathe. I need to appreciate. I need to act. I need to be grateful. I am. Now.

buck up camper

Dear me,

You need to stop being so analytical and criticizing yourself all the time! You are more special than you think, your boyfriend is into you and his family respects you for who you are. You don't need to compare yourself to the whores, you are pretty inside and out and need to FEEL THAT WAY. He doesn't look at other people! Everyone tells you that and even you have never seen him glance at another girl unless you point her out. So please stop making yourself sick with worry about your self-worth and if you are good for him. He thinks you are beautiful and will continue to be that way if you keep yourself up and continue to be happy with him.

You have needed this pep talk for a really long time. It's something that's long overdue. If you can see a person who you would assume to be unhappy and feel ugly and depressed and see them with a huge smile on their face and seemingly content then that's a smack in the face. All the people who are considered ugly that fall in love and make families; that just proves that real happiness is loving someone, yourself, and who you want to be. Your boyfriend loves you for who you are and wants you to just be happy with yourself for once so here's the kick in the ass to go do that.

Love yourself. That's my advice to anyone who actually read this. Never let anyone get you down.

Love,
the happy katie. _;D

To myself

It's time to let go.

Let go of the shit.

You got over depression and you're starting a great, but challenging senior year. Work hard and soon you'll be on your way through a pre-med college program.

So let go of the ex, who doesn't care about you anymore because he is distracted by drunken college life. Don't give him another chance. He's not worth it.

Let go of the boy, the boy you had twice and will never get again because he has a great girlfriend.

Let go of the asshole, the asshole who you know is only using you.

Just stop answering the texts.

Just stop.

If you need to feel like someone needs you, that's what all your friends and family are for. Let go of trying to be perfect. Stop letting people walk all over you. Stand up for yourself. Be you and don't be afraid to just say fuck off when needed. Stop giving people your time and effort who don't deserve it.

You are better than that.

You are so much better than that.

Dear...

Binge Eating Disorder,

We have been together for about a year now.

I have used you as an escape from stress, anger, and sadness. I have used you as a reason to fail. To self-sabotage. I have made myself sick thanks to you. I have hated my body, myself, and my lack of control.

But it's over.

We are done. I am done letting you control me.

I'm starting a new stage in my life, and I'm getting control over it without you, and without the food.

You won't be missed.

And no...I don't want to try and be friends now that we are through.

Thanks.

~S.

I'll see you in the mirror

Dear younger me,

It will be okay. I know right now you hurt, and trust me there will be much more hurt in your life, but know this; to feel pain is to know you're alive!

I know your heart hurts from getting it broken time and time again, but I promise there's a guy coming soon that will be worth all that pain. I can hear you saying, "how, how can all this pain possibly be worth it? It hurts so incredibly bad and I never want to feel this way again!" My simple reply is, get used to it. You will be hurt! But what I can tell you to ease that pain is that this guy is completely and 100% worth it.

He will hold you on your worst days and in that moment that he's holding you it will become the best day. He will treat you with more respect than any of those guys that you know now. He is passionate, not only about you, but about life and he will renew your passion for life just when you've hit lowest.

Now, don't go looking for him, time will bring him to you I promise. Be patient, I know you were never good at that.

Me

I Regret Nothing.

I took honors classes because I was bored. Yes, I'm smart. Yes, my GPA was 3.5 and higher my whole life. I have an amazing drive, anything I really I put my mind to I can do.

But did you ever stop and think that I don't WANT, I don't NEED to have some uber-amazing job and paycheck to be happy?

I was raised not having much, I was raised relying on the state for food and having to hear "We can't afford it." I know you want better for me but honestly, I don't regret not going to college. I don't need it. All I need is her. All I need is to know that I'm loved, that I have friends I can depend on, and that I can make enough to get by.

I don't regret anything I've done.

I'm the happiest I've ever been.

Dear Self,

I am so proud of you. You're taking initiative to better yourself. You are NOT going to let the anxiety and depression keep you down the way it has since you were 13. You are going to take the road to recovery with your binge eating, because you know your body cannot bear it any longer. You're going to stick to your medications, and carry through with the individual and group therapy that you've started, because although the social anxiety disorder makes you want to run, you KNOW that these people want to help you. They are not judging you, and they are not going to turn on you. You can't let your emotions rule what you eat and when. Your body needs something other than fats and sugars and carbohydrates, and in not-so-large quantities! You're about to be 19. You are too young to waste life lying in bed and stuffing yourself with trash. But you're starting to fix that, aren't you? I'm so proud of you. Please don't give up this time.

i've fallen down but i'm looking up.

You.

It's been a week and a half since I've self-harmed. I've gone to every class this week, an achievement for me. I've met someone new, someone who makes me smile so much that my friends can see such a difference in me.

It's weird; a week ago I was still miserable over you. I'm not saying I'm completely over you, because I know I'm not. But little by little you were fading back into the background. Until Wednesday when you looked at me and I caught your gaze and held it. It was only for a few seconds but it felt like forever until you looked away.

It was such a simple action and yet it lingers in my head. You made it clear to me you don't want me so why do you still look my way? I know I'm not imagining it; I'm not the only one who's noticed it. I'm trying really hard to move on but every man I meet I compare to you silently. It's not right. But I can't feel guilty, I just feel scared. What if this new guy is just like you?

I don't want to be used again. I'm keeping him at arm's length even though I feel like I could fall for him at any moment. I can't let myself do it, because you've made me trust no man, and besides, I don't want to be the girl who needs a man to validate her.

There are days when I think of you and I reach back for the knife...but I remind myself that I have to keep going. You're not worth the heartache and I have so much potential to be something more. Say your piece because I want to move on now.

I did fall down for a while. I may still be on the ground but I'm looking up.

Love, A xx

What I've learned about love thus far

Communicate- If someone is making you feel something, you should probably say something. It doesn't happen often. So don't waste something you crave so passionately. Let it be known

Move forward – What would be the point of life to regress? To do something over again when you in your heart know how it ends.

Let go – Baby it's time to let go. Move on. Set yourself free to find new love.

Love someone for who they are, not what you want them to be. Find someone who loves you for who you are, not what they want you to be.

Cry when it hurts – It's okay to feel. It's perfectly fine to be sad sometimes. You can't be so strong all the time. You're not a robot... as much as you want to be sometimes.

Don't lower your standards- Keep them high, don't settle for someone that doesn't deserve you. When the right one comes along... the standards won't matter.

Be true to yourself- because really, it's all we got in the end?

That's all that I've come up with so far. I still have so much to learn.

I realized something...

I need to love myself before I can accept that someone loves me.

I'm going to spend some time working on that, and just feeling good again.

I want to work out, and finally lose the weight that hangs over my head. I want to do it a healthy way, without obsessive calorie counting, starving myself, or anything else.

I want to get back into climbing, and swimming, and doing art again.

I want to start doing better in school, but not to the point I'm making myself sick over it.

I want to find who is important in my life, and just get away from the ones that hurt me.

I want to be able to look at myself in the mirror or in a picture and smile. Because I like myself.

I never want to doubt that someone loves me again, or that a guy could be interested in me. I'm tired of feeling like I'm not good enough.

I'm done. Things are changing.

Another Statistic.

I refuse to be another eating disorder statistic.
I refuse to be another obesity statistic.
I refuse to be another low self-esteem statistic.
Things are changing starting right this moment.
Not tomorrow, or next week, or next month. No, this minute. At
12:07am on Monday.

I refuse to count every calorie though, I know for me that isn't
healthy. It will lead to slowly cutting them out until I am not getting
enough. Or hating myself for having a certain number.

But I will start with just making sure I eat three normal sized meals a
day, plus a snack.

And work out, three times a week.

That seems like the healthiest way for me to go about this. I can't get
obsessive this way.

I want to be able to say, a few months from now, I don't have an
eating disorder.

I want to say it and not be lying to anyone.

I also want to say that I love myself. And that I am beautiful, and that I
am deserving of love.

For once.
I want things to change, and for once. I am going to follow this
through.
I'm done being a statistic.

I want.

I want to be happy. I want to live simply. I don't need things, things only complicate things. I want to live with no regrets. I don't want to look back on my life and wonder "what if?" I don't give a shit if no one else thinks I'm doing it the right way, I'm gonna live my life the way I want to. Fuck the world, I want to LIVE! I don't want to be in a box, a little comfortable house, with a wife, a dog and 2.5 kids. I want to be free, free to go where I want, do what I want. I guess most of all, I want to live for me, not my parents, not my family, not for the approval of my peers. I only need my own approval. I will blaze a trail that is my own. I will fuck up, I am NOT perfect! But, the mistakes I make will be mine, I will learn from them, I will grow, and be the person I am because of where I've been and what I've done. Who says fucking up is bad anyways? Edison didn't get the light bulb right the first time, and he was a fucking genius; so why the fuck am I expected to get everything right the first time? I will live the life I choose. I will be happy, I am blessed, I have clean air to breath, clean water to drink, and a roof over my head. I will rejoice in the little pleasures of life and lead the life that is waiting for me.

Remember

I just turned 25

I am a man

I am overweight

I am a recent survivor of cancer

As a result of my cancer treatments I might be diabetic

I currently live with my parents

I've Been to Rome.

I've seen Florence.

I've seen Venice.

I've been to Austria.

I've had REALLY good beer

I have performed on stage at Carnegie hall

I have seen the ocean

I have been horseback riding in the black hills of South Dakota

I have howled at the moon

I've been in love

I've had my heart broken

And I've broken hearts

I've lost family and friends

I've made new friends

I've had a one night stand

I've been to a strip club

I've read the bible cover to cover......it was confusing

I've lost my faith in god

I replaced that Faith with hope

I've cooked over an open fire

I've seen the sunrise

I've seen it set too

I've been stuck in the friend zone......many many times

I've been to Washington D.C.

I've argued about politics

I've decided i hate politics

I've taken a friend I secretly had a crush on a "friend date"..........on valentine's day...We're just friends

I've been to an Aerosmith concert
I've been to a Nine Inch Nails concert as well
I've learned how to play the guitar.......sort of
I've gazed at the stars.....i wish i had kissed her
I've realized that not kissing her is one of my biggest regrets.
I've been to Disney world
I've been back a few times
I've seen Van Gogh's "Starry Night"
I've been to Broadway and Times Square.
I've been propositioned by a hooker
I've never paid for sex....never will...unless you count breakfast the
next morning.
I've been the lead singer in a band
I've never gotten a speeding ticket
I've been to college.....didn't Graduate......yet
I've decided i'm going to be a chef
I'm going back to school in the fall to learn how.
you know i started this thinking it was going to be really depressing. i
was going to say something lame about how i wish i had someone to
share all this with.
but now, looking back at all of it remembering everything I've seen in
just 25 years, I'm suddenly excited about what life has in store for me.
my friends all tell me that i will meet an amazing woman someday.
I'm glad she hasn't met me yet.
The last year of my life has been spent dealing with cancer and chemo
and worry and blood and pain.
and I've spent it alone with my thoughts.
I've over-thought about my life
I've forgotten who i am
soon
very soon
I'll be that man again

Inspired by 'Remember'

I am 19.

I am a woman.

I have witnessed the hardest drug addicts.

I have been with the most spiritual people.

I have witnessed abuse, verbally and physically.

I've never been kissed or hugged or held hands with a guy.

Never been on a date either.

I am a virgin.

I have been drunk before.

I've smoked cigarettes before and quit cold turkey.

My longest relationship was 6 years.

I have had an online relationship before.

I have been homeless living with other people (mostly family) ever since I was born.

I was obese in middle school and what time I had in high school.

I have suffered through anorexia.

And haven't relapsed for 4 years.

But I have gained a heart problem due to it.

I have suffered through bulimia.

And haven't relapsed for 4 years.

But I have gained a broken rib bone, and lost my gag reflex.

I have refrained from cutting and burning myself for 2 years.

But I still have the scars.

I am a high school dropout due to my anorexia and bulimia.

But I'm going to college soon to get my Doctorates.

I taught myself to do better than what I was surrounded in.

I was bullied in most of the time I was at school.

I had my heart broken several times.

I broke hearts several times.

I've never been out of state, but I moved 11 times during fifth grade and first grade.

I've never been to Disney World.

I've never seen a concert before.

I am very strong Christian.

I've been at my most spiritual.

And I've been at the worst doubting and holding a grudge against God.

My friends are the best.

I have friends that are Wiccan, do hard drugs, cuss, Atheists, depressed, gay, lesbian, other ethnicities, are way older than me or way younger than me.

And through them I learn more than I could ever hope for or imagine.

They give me way more love than I could ever imagine.

I have not done drugs.

I have lived in the cheapest motels and trailers.

I have never lived in a house.

I have only been to a two story house once in my life.

I have almost drowned before.

I have fallen off a horse and got back up and rode again.

At age 5 I was abused physically, mentally, and verbally all in one day by my first babysitter and she told me not to tell anyone or she would kill my mom. Right when my mother got home, I told her every single detail.

I only see my father once a year if I'm lucky.

I have been bullied for being friends with someone of another race, another religion, or for being gay or lesbian.

I have met a billionaire before.

And at that moment I realized how I wanted to live my life.

Despite being through all this, I love every one of my friends, and stand up for them and help them when they're in need. Even if it goes against my moral values, my religious beliefs or if they look different. Because we all are the same. And I treat people the way I want to be treated. And despite going through all of this crap throughout my life, being tempted by drugs and sex and going through abuse and witnessing all this, I know when I move out and graduate college, I will be able to live a better life.

All you need is hope, faith, whatever. Don't give up on your life, it's yours and it's only once you get this. Stand strong, if you can't, endure to the end. Do not give up on yourself. You are the most important thing to you. You may not realize it right now, but you are what makes you happy. Do not go against yourself, don't hurt yourself. Just say, "I will get through this". Even if you do not believe it, even if you do not have a genuine feeling that it will get better. It will. Just keep saying it. Keep saying hopeful things; keep telling yourself you're strong. Because you are.

We are given this life to see how far we can go. With what we are given in life, whether it be poverty, abuse, being bullied, etc. etc. With that stuff we are given in life, we are sure to make it. Everyone has their problems, everyone has things that they think they won't get through but that's the moment when you stand up and shake it off. Because the obstacles you have are the ones that you can handle. Believe me. You can handle it and you can break through it. You just have to push yourself.

Do what you want, and don't judge yourself from where you come from or what you look like, you can do anything. And I know this is cheesy but, "Do your best, be your best, because you are the best!" I love you, world.

I can't be the only one.

My heart is this welcoming, generous, hopelessly romantic, all-encompassing thing that wants nothing more than to sit happily upon my sleeve, find the love of its life and spoil them rotten and treat them like a god. It loves everyone and everything, no matter how much hurt has been caused against it.

My brain on the other hand is an over analytical, dark, brooding, and sadistic fuck that loves nothing more than to watch my heart shrivel and shriek in pain while at the same time causing my stomach to churn and my body to shiver with insecurity and doubt. It has no soul and distrusts everyone it meets.

But my heart, for however loving and truly caring and wonderful it is, is also fairly resilient (or very, very stupid). It doesn't give up no matter how much my brain says it will. My heart will break and bleed and cry, but it will always find another someone to yearn for, someone to care for unconditionally for no other reason than its need to do so; even if the current object of my heart's affection does not have a heart that feels the same.

Fucked up, though the relationship between my heart and head may be, the only thing that will ever truly satisfy my brain is my heart being truly satisfied. Deep down, my brain wants to know love as much as my heart craves it.

This overwhelming sense of satisfaction is not only a nearly hopeless dream; it is also my greatest life goal.

My 19th year of being alive and breathing.

Sure, it sucked. It fucking SUCKED. And, technically, there's still time for it to suck more.

But we need to stop focusing on the negatives. All of us. These letters are like pieces of our souls, tiny parts of us that we feel we can't share. I've read letters to abusers, to rapists, to exes that broke the hearts of the letter-writers. I've read pleas for forgiveness, apologies, propositions, thank-yous; hell, I've written letters about most of these things too.

But, this is a new kind of letter for me. A letter about hope and relief. Because right now, while I'm sitting here in this tiny little room on this uncomfortable couch, watching that kitten sleeping and listening to my own heartbeat, I think I've discovered hope.

Because I've got so much more to do, in my 20th year. I've got so much more to do, in my tomorrow. Tomorrow will be my tomorrow, too. I'm going to face it head on, with my chin held high. It's mine now, nobody else's. I've got hope in my back pocket now and, dear reader, you should find yours and put it there.

Today I feel like dreaming

I feel like dreaming about the things that are to come, and the endless sea of possibilities that I have yet to discover. It is a wonderful feeling to know that anything you can dream in life, with some effort, some vision and a little bit of luck can be achieved.

I have just graduated from college and I am about to start my working life, my career. Feelings of all kinds invade me. Questions bug my mind constantly, would I be able to be successful? Would I be able to be a leader? Would people look up to me and place their trust in me? I am going to find out, and tonight I feel like dreaming that I can do what I set my mind to do, that I am capable of beating my fears and reach my goals.

I am also in love, and it is with a girl that I consider the woman of my dreams. She is so pretty, and she has a smile so radiant and vivid like no other. Her long black hair fascinates me to no extent and her soft white skin mesmerized me since the first moment I touched it. Tonight I feel like dreaming that I would be able to overcome all the obstacles set by life, so I can be with her. I feel like dreaming that it doesn't matter how difficult or unlikely the situation we are living in, is. With the power of will, perseverance and love we can someday be together.

Tonight I will close my eyes and let my dreams take me to a world where anything can happen, hoping that in the morning when I open them, I will wake up with renewed strength, ready to give this convoluted mess that I call my life, my best shot.

Holy Shmoles

I have so much to be thankful for, and I just fully realized it.

I had like a major thankfulness epiphany.

I have so many things to do this week, but when I stopped to think about the current status of my life, I am so happy. There's no rush to do anything, I don't know why I worry about little things. I am 20 years old, there are so many opportunities ahead of me.

So I hope when you think of your life status, it makes you feel warm and joyful.

I feel as if the joy is a ball of fire, aching and yearning to erupt from inside me and spread joyfulness everywhere. But instead, I keep it contained, right at bursting point. I can feel its heat coursing through my body. Who could be stressing with a feeling like that?

And I may not have a billion friends, but the friends I do have are really really great and give me much joy. They understand!

I assure you I'm not under the influence of anything either, this is real.

Declaration To Be.

This is my declaration to you, Claud. My declaration to be brave, to be an adult, but most importantly to be honest to myself.

I've loved you since we were 15. Since the days of innocent games, and silent stares over our notebooks. I loved you while you held me, drowning in despair. I loved you when "Fix you" was not only our song, but our anthem. I've loved you while you've been childish, while you've been funny, while you've been sad. Every day, when I realised you weren't going to call me again, when you had to ignore me, when you made my soul, the one you so tenderly cared for, break, I loved you still.

But here is my declaration from me to myself:

You Claud, are worth more than the sobs, than the tearing hole in your chest. You are worth more than the feelings of rejection and heartbreak. Even in the darkest of hours, you've held onto your strength, your very core. Continue to do so. You are more than the boy who broke your heart.

Dear ball of stress (aka, me),

Get yourself together. Don't stress out. You'll get everything done.

Breathe. In, out. In, out.

Don't procrastinate and you'll be fine. You'll be fine...just chill out, and break it up into pieces.

Focus. Focus...don't give in to the urge to talk to the one you want to; don't go check things you "need" to. You know you really don't, but what you do need to do are the tasks at hand.

Rein in the anger, the tears, and don't worry – just work. You can do it.

Work on the smallest one first; its deadline is closest, too. Pick yourself up, and set to work. It will be easy.

You'll be fine!

Letters to my Mind

Dear Mind,

Stop.

Stop what you're doing to me, it's unfair and you know it.

Please, let me eat. It's okay. It's okay to eat.

Please, let me smile. It's okay. Smiling is supposed to happen.

I am meant to be happy, I need to be happy, and what you are telling me right now isn't making me happy.

Stop yelling my flaws at me. They don't exist. Everyone has flaws, everyone is imperfect, and that's what I like. I love the imperfection, so stop trying to "make things right".

Stop blaming me for things. I didn't do anything you blame me for.

Nothing.

Mind, you are starving me from my life. You are making me lack the happiness and fulfillment I used to feel. What is happening? Why has our friendship turned into hatred?

All I am asking is that you let feelings in. Maybe you should become more acquainted with my heart, work things out together. Because right now, I need you to be positive, I need you to be there for me. I need you to help my body function and uplift my mood.

I need you to work this out.

Love,
Me

I am strong.

I am strong. I can do this. I will do this. I will be a good mother. I will treat my child right. I can and will do the hard things that need to be done to be a good person.

You are one of those hard things. I am cutting you out of my life. I love you, but I will not let you treat me like that anymore. I gave you a chance to straighten up, I know that you aren't yourself with her, but you ran all over that chance.

Now I'm done.

I have been raped.

I have been used.

I have been manipulated.

I have been abused.

I have been through the harder things in life, and I am strong.

Now I'm pregnant, at 17, with your child.

I will do this too.
I am strong. I know it will take every ounce of my strength to do this, but you will not treat me badly anymore. I do not deserve it. I am a good person.

And I swear to you if you decide to be involved in your child's life and you do not treat us right you will not have the right to see your child anymore.

I am strong for myself.
I am strong for my future child.
I am strong to keep hope in a brighter future for my child.

Do Better

To the person that I am right now:

What are you doing with your life? Do you see what is wrong with yourself? Because everyone else does.

1. Your eating habits have GOT to go. You are headed down the path of anorexia. You are losing weight. But you aren't fat. This is not good.
2. Work harder in school. I know that you hate it and you legitimately find it hard and really don't think that it is worth much. But I'm pretty sure it is. I bet you your future that it will be worth it in the end.
3. The sadness. I'm not sure what causes it or that there even always is a cause. But do something about it. Tell someone, look for help, anything. Because it is not doing you any favors.
4. Get birth control. Stop having sex just because he wants it. I think you get the point.
5. Be happy. In the end that will get you the farthest and be the best. Do better than you are doing now. It's for the best. I promise.

(From the person I am right now who wants to do better)

a letter to myself.

Dear Me,

Why do you have to be so hard on yourself? Almost everyone around you thinks you're nice, funny, smart, and beautiful. Why can't you just see it?

Why are you constantly second guessing yourself and every decision you make? I wish you knew how to have a less negative attitude. Why do you constantly cause yourself extra anxiety, pain, and stress?

I know why you have so much self-doubt; nothing's ever been easy for you. I know how much it hurt having no one to talk to for years. Which is what makes it so nerve-wracking to talk to people now.

I know how much it sucks having to bottle away every thought, emotion, and fear. Why can't you let people in?

I know how depressed you are, and I am afraid for what you may do if you keep going down this road. Life is meaningless to you, but I know you don't want death. You just want happiness.

Why won't you let yourself have it?

I know there's an amazing person deep down inside there somewhere... You see glimpses of her at times, but when will you just let her out?

(Please try to) love,
yourself

To My Future, and The Future as a Whole

I struggle to work out the anxiety about it. I've always wanted to be the best, to be in the ivies, to get a good job, to make a lot of money and have a beautiful family. I'm only fifteen. It drives me insane.

I've decided, future, I will be a doctor. Although I still want to go to an Ivy League school and attend the best medical school possible this decision has eased some of my pain. What I want is to help people; I want to become an oncologist. I will do all I can to keep your family and loved ones alive, with you and to never see a tear shed from a death by cancer.

I have never once been rejected or failed at anything I truly wanted. I won't lose now, to my future and the future as a whole – I'm going to be here, I'm going to save you and I'm going to make a difference. I just pray to god I'm strong enough.

Life.

Lately, I feel like I'm breaking down. There's just too much to do and too little time, with less money than necessary and little to no outside support. I didn't have to choose to be their father. I don't have to be your rock. I wish you'd quit blaming me for things I can't help, can't change, or just don't notice.

Regardless, I know everything is gonna be okay. I don't know when, or how, but I know all we have to do is stick together. Everything else is just a speed bump.

A letter to myself...

Pull yourself together. You feel alone in your search for who you are, where you belong, and what you will be.

Don't compare yourself to anyone else. You are unique. It's ok if you don't have a perfect face, if you aren't a size 0.

You can embrace your quirky sense of humour, your intelligence...don't second guess yourself. It's ok to make mistakes; it's ok to have flaws. NO ONE IS PERFECT. Be nicer to yourself, let things go. Do not define yourself by a grade, an action, a criticism....or through anyone else.

Don't fall for any boy that shows you attention. You need to value what you are, and what you have to offer. You deserve to feel loved, and to love in return. At the same time, NEVER let a man define you.

You are allowed to feel scared, nervous, vulnerable, unsure....just remember that every day offers new opportunities, and room to learn and grow.

You may not have all the answers, but have faith in yourself...you will figure it out.

To myself.

You need to let go. Of yourself, your fear, and the little insecurities that you hold so close to home. You need to realize that you have friends, potential lovers, and the prospect of a good life. You need to realize that everything that was said and done was because he was drunk, and whether or not he meant them aside, the things he said shouldn't affect you as an adult now. You need to grow up a little and learn to deal with things and move past them. If you don't you are going to feel alone for the rest of your life, just as you do now.

I wish I could say with love, but we aren't there yet.
- Yourself.

A new path

The clouds of confusion are finally clearing and I can begin to see the light through the storm. I have one friend who helped me more then she could ever know. I will simply say I cannot thank her enough and I doubt she even knows what or how much what she did helped me. So thank you and don't doubt what you have and take the plunge with him. You two are great together.

I think I can finally say I am ready to go back to where I live and soon enough back home. If I hadn't worked out most of my issues I don't believe I could have continued functioning in my life. I'm so happy that I have finally stopped having the suicidal thoughts that were racing through my head for so long. Nearly 6 months in a state where every day I thought about how I could go about doing it. I thought about going and buying a pistol. I thought about the knives in my kitchen, the knives in my gear, I thought about jumping off the building so many times. Surprisingly enough even typing that out I don't get those thoughts about doing it but rather how I am so glad I never tried. I've spent my life constantly repressing everything emotional out of fear of showing weakness but it occurs to me that I don't need to cover up everything to keep up appearances. Everyone has a degree of fucked up things in their life and if they bottle it up they only make life a whole lot harder and a lot more fucked up. (To my friend sorry I didn't tell you I was having those thoughts back then but I couldn't)

I've started to pray every day and I don't know if it is working or if it just happens to be good timing. I would like to think that it is working and that god is finally allowing me to have a full life. I am also trying to be a much nicer person. I was always sort of an asshole before but now I need to be a better person. Here it is! I will try to not only better myself but also the people around me!

To God. Thank you for the people you have put in my life to help me, without them I wouldn't be here now and please help me to stay on this path. I don't know if I could handle going back down the path I am coming from.

Well if you read this far thanks... I needed to say things I can't tell people.

-s

Dear Body

I just want to say sorry. I'm sorry that I hated you and hurt you for so long. I'm sorry that I didn't realise sooner how beautiful and perfect you are right now, not 5 pounds or 10 miles from now. I hurt you in so many ways, from starving you, stuffing you and working you until you screamed in pain. No matter how much weight I lost, I always wanted you to look better. I expected you to somehow make my life better and fix all of my problems. I am finally starting to learn to treat you the way you deserve by feeding you and letting you rest when you need to. I'm sorry if I mess up from time to time and hurt you still. It's a long road to recovery but I'm willing to fight in order to protect you. Body, you allow me to experience my life and that is the most that I can ever ask for from you. Thank you for being amazing just the way you are. <3

Substance for Substance

Me,

Who am I? Who are you? You've lost all your substance to a substance. You've allowed it to take it all; tangible and otherwise. The property is minor, but you can't even find yourself. Where did you go?

Are you somewhere down there? I've spent six months looking with not a clue in sight. I'm getting impatient and I need you back. I need to live life; MY life and I don't even know what that is.

I need to know what you need to be happy. I need you, me. So give me a hint, a clue to stop being blue. We've got to get this life of ours together. It's got to be whole before we can share it with the most beautiful girl in the world.

I've chased away the substance and I need me back.

Love,
You

This is a letter to my younger self.

Well. I know. Life sucks right now. You're most probably crying into a pillow, wishing you weren't fat.

YOU'RE NOT FAT. Sweetheart, you're 12 years old and you weigh approx. 5 and a half stone. Don't listen to those ridiculous people, they're jealous, they don't realise that one day, you're gonna own their asses in any beauty competition.

Your confidence is low. You need to get right on top of the world again, you're amazing when you know what you want, you just won't stop till you get it, and that's a really good quality to have.

When you're 16, you'll meet a guy.

This guy will be the most amazing person you've ever met. he'll make you laugh, he'll make you feel loved, he'll call you beautiful and mean it, he'll be the best thing that ever happened to you. And you know, it isn't young love. It's real.

One day, you won't remember why you love him.

The world will start to feel dark; you'll feel more alone than ever.

But you have to remember, remember when you first met, the kiss in the snow, under the lamppost, in the middle of London.

Remember how he cries after you. He cares for you more than any other person ever could.

He's the reason the sun shines. The sugar in your tea. The key to your heart.

You're the lonely girl who's forgotten how to love, sweetheart this is your time to remember, you adore him.

Let me be myself

Dear self,

I'm writing to inform you that you are a wimp. Why didn't you kiss her that night outside her front door? The look she gave you was a dead giveaway.

Why are you the nice guy? Probably because you have nothing to offer other than your wry cynical mannerisms and your pseudo-intellectual, and you desperately seek the attention. It's a shame that it hasn't worked yet.

"If not now, then when" is the saying you tell yourself before making any sort of titanic decision. That is what motivates you? It's pathetic. Maybe you should just pack it up and accept where you are and where you are going. Granted, you may be smart and have the ability to do well in an educational environment, but who cares? In two or three more years no one is going to care what you got for a grade in a chemistry course.

You say you want to be a doctor, and I have faith in you. Let go of everything that holds you down whether it be your mind, your body, women, men, drugs, anxiety, or your depression. Take all of those negative aspects and turn them into fuel for reaching your ultimate goal. You are in pain. Why not get a reward for your suffering? Your pain is a gift.

You may not know me or you may not want to, but all I have to say, from one to another, is let me be myself.

Advice for my younger self,

Don't forget to stop and smell the roses.

Remind your friends and family you love them as often as you can.

You meet loves of your life multiple times. It's timing that dictates who is THE love of your life.

Dance around your room every now and then.

Love yourself, you are beautiful.

Whenever you fail a test, just remind yourself that school is overrated. The world would be a much better place if people were compassionate and stupid versus selfish and educated.

You'll never be the best; you'll never be the worst.

Every year we reflect on the previous year and think how stupid we were. It's unavoidable, so don't be upset. Laugh it up.

Surrender

Every day I feel like I am on the verge. On the verge of being happy...on the verge of finally letting go...on the verge of forgiving myself and others....on the verge of loving myself. I want so badly to cross over, to allow myself to fall head first into happiness, love, forgiveness, loneliness, peace. Something keeps me on the verge though, I don't know what exactly; could be feelings of inadequacy, of apathy, of imperfection- as if falling off the verge and into life will create this mess, this chaotic sequence of events that I can't control. I want chaos...I want messy love, I want to be so happy that I get deep wrinkles on my cheeks, I want to live in every sense of the word. I don't want these numbers in my head anymore, I don't want the guilt of nourishing myself. I want my throat to be worn down by good wine and deep, body shaking laughter, not by acid. I want rich hair, and vibrant skin. I want my teeth to fall out when I'm old, after having eaten good food and told thousands of stories, not because they eroded. I love my bones because make me, me, but I don't want to make them brittle. Life is so beautiful and I want my body to be here for years and years to take me everywhere, to love as much as I can. I am deciding now to control my thoughts and not let them control me. To become healthy. To live.

What I learned at 18

Dear Life,

I guess you're a popular guy, I don't know when this letter will reach you or if it will ever be read, hopefully it helps somebody.

You have taught me so many things and in the strangest ways, don't eat fish unless you know who cooked it and how, or else you might just die. Don't go to parties with people you think you know because of work. Always be kind, in every situation because you never really know how small the world is.

I think the best thing I can say I have learned is that, the hardest thing to be is yourself. Everybody has an opinion on who you should be, or who you are. They tell you what to do with your life, what your talents are, I'm sure if you let them they would draw you a diagram, label it, laminate it, and most likely they would tape it to your forehead, just so you never lose it.

I was led to believe that I knew what was right for me, and that I was living my own life. That is correct, right? I guess what I'm trying to say is that I have learned a lot. I often think "what is going on with me?" I guess you could call it growing up. I enjoy who I am, and I cherish all of my decisions, even the "so stupid, I can't believe I did that" ones. I prayed to God a few times, you guys are pretty close right?

This year has been a year of firsts, I do anything and everything now. I don't want to miss out on anything, but I also know that it's okay to skip some things.

I have found love in many people, I don't know if it was meant to be but if it is we will meet again.

I have learned to love myself, I think I'm beautiful and I don't care if you think that's cocky sounding. It has taken me so long to feel this way, I always felt empty and lost, it took me 18 years but I am more than ready to live the fullest out of life.

Thank you from the tips of my toes to the top of head.

Love,
Me

Me, Yes, Me

Dear Past Self,

I have learned a lot and am still learning every day. I am definitely not perfect nor will ever want to be. Here is what I wished you would have known years ago. Months ago. Even days ago.

I wish you would have realized how amazing and beautiful you are early on.

You may be...
The one who always had some other girl picked over her.
The one who always had someone better than her around.
The one who had to listen to the insults every day.
The one who was never skinny enough.
The one who was never pretty enough.
The one who was never loved.
The one who was so sheltered from the world.
The one who could never do anything right.
The one who was always seen as just a friend.
The one who never spoke.
The one who was always the good girl.
The one who will die a virgin.
That just because he didn't want you, doesn't mean you have to makeover yourself completely.

Everything you do, do for yourself. Find the confidence you've never had.

Because you have those individuals you want to prove wrong. Those you want to make angry. Those that hurt you and left scars on and inside you. You want them to feel regret? You want to piss them off? To get revenge?

The only way to do that is to be the best you you can be.

Stop comparing yourself to your friends. Who cares if you think they're smarter, prettier, skinnier, or have a boyfriend. There should be no competition. The only person you need to worry about is yourself. Forget about the times where you've considered how everyone would feel if you were gone. Where you've considered ending your life. Thought of the easiest most painless ways you could do it. Crying yourself to sleep because no one seemed to care about you that night. Because one day you will have your perfect fairytale. It may start in just a few days, weeks, or years. It may come at the end of your life. But you will find that perfect ending.

Now quit the crying, whining, and living with the regrets in the past. You may not have him, but there will be plenty more in the future. Ones who actually care this time. One who treats you right. One who is so amazing and who's so imperfectly perfect for you. One who will be your closest best friend and love you for every day of your life.

He does exist. He's just somewhere out there.

You may have no idea how to get to where you want in life, but you'll somehow make it one day. No matter how many times you'll get lost. You've worked hard enough for it.

Because you are the girl with the worst luck. Yet, I know one day, this luck will turn around because you absolutely positively deserve it.

Now forget the bump in your nose, that your thighs are too big, that you're the last virgin on earth, or that you can't even jog a quarter of a mile without being out of breath.

Just remember this most of all...you are such a beautiful, intelligent, and unique individual, and you don't even realize it.

ah, life. it's a bitch.

To the me that thinks she isn't worth it,

You will always have days that make you wonder why you were put on this earth. You will always wonder if you have done enough. You will always have days where life sucks. You will always want it to get better. You will always have days when you just want to give up.

When you have those days, just remember: you are worth everything to a lot of people. The days that make you wonder why you were put on earth are the days that will help you grow. Those days will help you to walk along side another person who is struggling.

When you wonder if you've done enough, the answer is always yes. You are a perfectionist. You never give up unless you have tried everything. And when you do give up, it's not because you want to, it's because you care so much that you have to let it go. It has to be enough.

On the days when life sucks, just remember that you are blessed beyond belief. You have a wonderful family, both biological and chosen. You have a roof over your head and clean clothes to wear every day. You have the ability to do as you please. You have friends that care deeply about you. You are blessed with the ability to read and write. You are getting a college education, something that many people only dream about having. You have everything you need and lots of things that you want. You are set apart by God, chosen for a specific purpose that only you can fulfill.

Those days that you want to get better? Well, guess what. They will. The sun always shines the next day. It may not always be obvious, but life is good. Do you know why? You are alive. Out of all the people on the face of the earth, you are still alive. Even if everything isn't okay now, it will be in the end. If it's not okay, then it's not the end.

Please, please don't give up. I know that some days will be overwhelming, but you have to keep on going. You have to. I can promise you that things will be better. Looking at the past, I can see how far you've come and you have so much farther to go.

All of this is just to say that you are perfect just the way you are. Absolutely perfect. Your life is worth it. You are worth it. You may not always believe it, in fact, you may never believe it, but I can see it now. Everything that you are, everything that you can be, everything that you will be is perfect. It. Is. Worth. It. I promise. In the end, I know you'll be able to see it too.

Love yourself. Love your life. It's the best thing you can do.

Love, the wiser me

Wake-up Call

Dear Self,

I wish you would get out of this rut you are in. Remember when you were so happy and everything was fine? Alot has changed from then, but YOU ARE STILL FINE. So why are you unhappy? Why do you get so lonely when there are so many people around you? Why do you not have the confidence to show people who you are? You have a beautiful man who is completely in love with you, yet you take it for granted. You have been through many changes lately, but you made it through. The hard part is over. Wake up! Life is passing you by!

I love YOU!

I sat here thinking about what I want to write because there's so much I want to get off my chest. I thought about maybe writing about my bf and how much he changed my life (for the better), I've thought about writing about my Dad and how much I miss him since he's passed. Maybe writing about my mother and how I wish she had the will power to change her life because she deserves so much better despite the shit she's done. And even to my brother, and how I wish I could give him the power to stay strong through all the bullshit...

But really...I want to write about how I feel right now. This letter is to myself.

Good job dealing with all that bullshit. Here's a pat on the back for finally seeing the positive side of life, and that's such a huge accomplishment! You went through that that terrible storm of bullshit, disappointment, misery and let downs, but here you are. You're still alive.

None of that worrying and stress even mattered! All you needed to do was worry about YOU!

Congrats for changing your mindset, because not many people can do that. Way to go for rising above. Here's to the praise and love you never got from them. You finally found it within yourself.

I love you. You are an amazing, beautiful, intelligent person and you have come so far. Way to go!

Love,

YOU!

The Word Today

The word today is struggle; because it is the one word I have always competed with and have never conquered. No spelling test, essay or speech could properly overcome this word and no test can put it to rest.

It is not failure. The B received in Chemistry is not a failure; it is only a future struggle for medical school. The boyfriend lost on my birthday is not a loss, but a struggle to maintain order and peace in life. My dog being sick is a struggle, my health failing is a struggle, my family dying is a struggle, my body is a struggle, life is a struggle.

The word tomorrow is hope

I have not been able to put hope in a sentence with failure, loss, or misery. My life is full of hope. My body has hope, my family has hope and my med school future plans have hope. Hope for better grades, for better ability to focus. Hope for someone who will show me respect and love me always. Hope for my family, that they will persevere, that life will continue

The word today is struggle
Tomorrow there is hope
struggle to find hope
then hope

Me

You,

I want to let you in on a little secret......

YOU ARE AMAZING!!

You may not feel it right now but you truly are spectacular. You brighten up people's day even if you don't know it.

You are strong and you can weather the storm. Life is hard but don't ever let it get you down because someone somewhere needs you.

Keep on smiling my friend because you are beautiful!!

Love,

Me

Apologies to my 13 year old self...

You're almost 20 now. I'll be honest, life is pretty good. But there are some things I feel I need to apologise to you for, darling.

My biggest apology is that you still haven't found that sweet, practically first true romance you're always dreaming about. You'll be dreaming about that for at least the next 6 years, I'm afraid. I can't tell you why. If we knew that, I wouldn't be apologising to you for it right now.

My next apology is that there are still a lot of things you wish to do that I haven't done yet. Like learn the guitar, or the piano (although you will meet a friend who will start teaching you, but you're not there yet). Or get the lead role in a play – you'll have some roles, but you're still not good enough yet for them, no matter how hard you try.

I must also apologise for that lack of confidence you have in yourself, in your looks. You'll have those for a couple of years more until you get the skin treatment you needed, the braces finally off, and the confidence, through being forced to get up in front of a class of bitchy girls and perform your dance. Don't worry though, they might judge, but they don't say anything.

What I won't apologise to you for, however, is who and where you are now, what you have. Sure, you still haven't really had a first boyfriend yet, and it kills you every day inside, no matter how much you listen to Queen's "Somebody in Love", no prince charming has come along yet. But that aside, you're in your second year at your top choice uni, doing the subjects you love. You're living in your own house now too! With, quite frankly, extremely awesome people who you should hopefully be friends with beyond university. You still get on amazingly well with your parents. Your friends are different, but some have stuck around from back then. Some you don't know yet, but you will very soon and they too are still in your life and you love them very much, they helped you become the girl you truly are, and that girl got you here today, typing on her laptop to you at midnight in her own bedroom, in her own house, at her top choice uni, 2 weeks before her 20th birthday. She's not smiling, but she's happy.

Good job

Dear Self,

You tried and failed, but I'm really proud of you for trying.
Try more.
Fail better.
Always love yourself.
Now go to bed.

xoxo

Persistence

I've been through a lot in my 20 years on earth.

I've dealt with losing a parent, having a gay parent, weight issues, drugs, losing close friends and family members, depression, bipolar disorder, and social awkwardness.

People take so much for granted. The impermanence of our existence is beautiful and simultaneously heart-breaking.

At times I question why I persist? I've been trampled over many times before. I've been ignored, ridiculed, spited, betrayed, ostracized, and intentionally hurt for fun. I can't find a decent girl, a reliable friend, or a wise mentor. My life is in shambles at the moment. Yet I maintain a positive attitude.

I may never understand people but I refuse to be one of the ones society tramples underfoot and leaves lost and confused. I will reject that notion and be one that rises above society; its values, its morals, its standards. I will be everything you hate; free-spirited, rebellious, compassionate, and fearless.

I won't be afraid to stand up and disagree with what's wrong with the world. I won't let you scare me into obeying you. I will care for my brothers and sisters like you won't; there will be no violence, no prejudice, no hatred in my heart. I will do the things I want to do if I feel they are right with me.

You can take your religion, your politics, your wars, your racism, your "morals", your hypocrisy, and your propaganda.

...and you can go fuck yourself.

I will not be silenced, I will not be tamed, I will not be controlled.

Shun me, ridicule me, despise me.
I will persist.

Ms.

This is a letter to myself whenever I think life is too hard. My letter of gratitude:

I am grateful that I'm alive and healthy
I am grateful for my daughter
I am grateful for my family
I am grateful for the fact that I am one of few women who had the means to leave an unhappy marriage
I am grateful that I finally fell in love with someone in such a passionate way
I am grateful for the circumstances of this last year, which despite bringing me to depths I'd never known possible, have forced me to listen to my soul and make changes that will bring me peace
I am grateful for my profession that I love and am stimulated by
I am grateful that I can pursue happiness
I am grateful for the warmth of my home
I am grateful for my comfortable bed

Life is a journey with no final destination (maybe the final destination is death) – it's experiences, learning, heartaches, challenges, discoveries, feeling good, feeling shit. It's a constant struggle to keep the balance between the yin and yang. So when things get tough and you wonder what the hell this is all for, I tell myself to stop wondering and just live; just feel; just be.

I had a dream we went away....

The world is a sad, confusing place. So many things are going wrong. Everyone has problems and I don't know how to fix them — I can't even wrap my head around my own, which aren't even a fraction of what other people in my life are experiencing right now. It's extremely exhausting and frustrating — I just want to stop all of the hurt, all of the confusion, all of the pain, all of the suffering. I want everyone to be happy; I want everything to go right. But I can't make that happen. It's life and things will go wrong, people will get hurt, et cetera. It's just been so much lately, so hard to shake. I guess I'll just have to keep holding on. Blue skies will come again.

Reflection

You—

your life is not pre-determined for you, and I hope that you realize that and fully understand it each and every day. You do not have to live the life your parents live, and you do not have to live the life society expects you to live. You have a strong heart, a hard head and a positive attitude- SO GET OUT THERE AND CHANGE THE WORLD. Your passion is evident; you just need to let it shine. Remember that money, appearance and status are only trivial issues in the big picture of life. Follow your dreams, chase after your goals, and go where the wind takes you. And while you embark on this journey of life, remember the people who helped you get there and the people who will continue to be by your side. You have a gift for surrounding yourself with amazing people; don't let those people slip away, they are vital to your success. Trust yourself always, but do not let those little insecurities you have about the way you feel get to you; they can destroy you if you let them. Never forget that perseverance is key and that without the bad times, the good times would not be so sweet. Put others before yourself when possible, but remember that you are human too and sometimes your own interests need to be accounted for. Every once in a while your optimistic self will stumble upon a bad day, and guess what? That's perfectly okay. Embrace it. Without the occasional bad day, the good days would not be as sweet. Welcome change with open arms and understand that it's inevitable. Don't ever let anyone tell you what to believe, and when the time and urge strikes- speak your mind, peacefully and eloquently. Don't ever think that what you believe now will be what you believe forever. As you grow up, your beliefs and values will change with the experiences life presents you; let this happen. Your life is just beginning; however no one knows when it will end. So start today, take control, and breathe in deep. This is your life. LIVE IT.

Love. Always and Forever.
—You

It's okay

Dear Me,

It's time to get your shit together. You've been through a lot these past couple months but what you're dealing with will only make you a stronger person in the future. You're worried and feel helpless. In some cases you feel completely depressed. You've been abandoned. The friends you once trusted more than any of the others are the people who have let you down the most; besides yourself. You're better than this. You deserve better than this and you know how to achieve what you want.

Don't make life decisions based on what you think is easy. Learn to strive for something. Things have always come easy for you but that's over now. You're an adult. Start acting like one. Grow up. The realization that you can no longer sit on your ass and expect everything to work out is hitting you now. Deal with it. Deal with the fact that you're going to need to put effort into your future to get the things you want. Forget the people that you once loved and focus on the plans you have with the ones you love now. Don't forget what's important to you. Things will get better. Stay on task and get out of school. That's where your life should truly begin. Suck it up for now. Enjoy what you have and don't regret what you've missed out on. What is meant to be will be. You have a reason for being here. Find it. You'll be okay, even when it feels like you won't be.

You have people that love you unconditionally. Don't take them for granted. They're what matters. Keep only the close friendships that feel you cannot live without; the ones that prove that they deserve to stay apart of your life forever. Fighting never solves anything. Don't waste your time on petty arguments. They're not worth it. Tell someone when they piss you off. How will they know not to do that again if they don't understand that it bothered you before? The people you know are not mind readers. They're human. Just like you. Everyone makes mistakes. You should know this well. It's not the mistake that matters; it's the next move. How you correct your mistake is where you show your true character.

Don't take life so seriously. It's not like you're getting out alive. Appreciate your elders. They've been through more of life. They have more experience. Listen. You may be lucky enough to learn something from them. You've been a good kid. Take your childhood, fold it up, and keep it as a reference. Look back only to admire, never regret. You are a good person. Change someone's life in an unexpected way before you die. You have a future. Don't mess it up. Stay on track and follow through. Paint for fun. Have fun. You may be an adult but let lose when necessary. Know when it's necessary. You will be okay. Know that.

love always,
Yourself

Hello past/hi future

Hello past...

This is me saying goodbye — thanks for the lessons, but goodbye. Goodbye to painful memories, shame, humiliation and feelings of worthlessness — I AM DONE with you. I am finished re-living voices that hurt me, told me lies, and made me doubt myself. While I know that you happened for a reason, and I appreciate the wisdom that you now gave me, I am done....you are a friend I no longer need.

Hi future,

I want you to know I am finally ready for you — ready to be open to whatever you will bring. I'm not scared of failing, rejection, change or pain because I know it will all lead to something wonderful. I hope you hear this so that you pick up a little bit of speed (I need you to bring some sparks back into the everyday life...) — so that I can feel the magic again. Can't wait to meet you tomorrow! Look out for me okay? I'll be here! And I'll make you proud.

Hey present,

Thanks for bringing me to where I am now, with my family, in a place of new beginnings and possibilities. I feel lucky to be here and to have arrived in one piece — it is so peaceful to feel whole. I promise to remember to be thankful for you, not waste my time with you on looking to the past, but spend it enjoying you, now. I promise myself and you to focus on the beauty around me, the people beside me, and the life within me. I'm glad I'm here with you.

I am My Own Worst Enemy

Today is the day. Rather, tonight is the night. The night I say goodbye to the girl I have been.

I am done being the girl who hates herself.

The girl that cries because she eats.

The girl with scars on her wrists.

The girl that cheats on her wonderful, doting boyfriend to feel wanted.

The girl that drinks more than people realize.

The girl that is terrified of what she is becoming.

I want to be the girl that my friends see. I want to be worth everything they think I am. I'm done being scared. I don't want to hate myself anymore. I want to see the beauty they tell me is there. I am a 21 year old woman and I am strong. It might not all be perfect tomorrow, but damn sure I am going to try every day.

I can't wait for tomorrow.

For You Troubled Soul

For you, Troubled Soul,

This world is a difficult place sometimes. It is full of hardships and heartbreak. Maybe it's the loss of a loved one. May it's the loss of the heart. Maybe it's the loss of yourself. Maybe it's a loss others cannot comprehend. Regardless,

the world feels like it's against you.

You wonder how you'll recover, or how you'll fill the empty space...the one the loss left. How will you rebound? How will you be the person you once thought you were? You think every day, when will these hardships end?

Why is the world picking on me?

Troubled Soul, it may seem like the Earth is your bully and you its number one victim. But remember, you are not alone. There are others with pain, maybe exactly like yours or maybe different. Yet, you all share the same thing and that is pain.

You my friend must remember that the world will keep on spinning. Time will keep going and this soon will all be in the past. As for now, you need to make the best of the worst and keeping on living.

Present You, is doubtful because the pain seems endless.

Future You is thankful. Why? Because these hardships you face now are the ones that make you who you are.

You are an incredible human being because though life may be rough, you live through every day.

The losses you have now will be gains in your future. Be the best you can be. Don't let anything or anyone tell you otherwise.

And always remember, every soul on this Earth has love to give. You says you can't have some of it?

I'll see you soon,

Future You

Keep on Keepin' On

Wow, this has been a hard period in my life.

I am amazed at how it keeps piling up and piling up – all the bills, all the madness, all the stress – it's so overwhelming. There are days when I am so low but I keep pushing through. I have to keep going. I have to keep focused. I have to take those steps forward because at least then I'm getting somewhere, regardless of how slowly.

Hate to break it to me...but this period may last for a long time. Yes, self, I know that's hard to hear. I may have to change my plans along the way. I may not get my perfect outcome. I may have to redefine what I consider success. And (grab a hankie) I may fail.

I need to keep moving forward. Even if it's baby steps, they're still steps. Even when I get knocked down, just take a breather, dust myself off and move forward.

It doesn't need to be huge steps...it just needs to be forward.

I can do it.

I trust me.

A
LETTER
TO
YOU

Hope

We don't search for love. The world has always thought that love is what every soul capable of loving strives for. To find that significant other, to find that one person who knows the ins and outs of our mind, body, and soul. That person or object that we can laugh with, smile towards, raise an eyebrow to, and bite our lip whenever we see them. The butterflies of it all, the nervous anticipation of a text or call, the anger and disappointment when things don't quite go the way you had hoped it would. This is what most think we strive for. In the truest sense, we strive for hope. We hope that one day we will find that one person that looks at us with as much passion, care, and love as we do when we look at them. We hope that we find that person, and we hope we are smart enough to hold on to them. We hope that we can pick out the real ones from the wrong ones, because we are tested in every sense when it comes to finding what we thought we strive for. False looks, false hope, false love. The nastiest and toughest lesson we all learn to face is within our heart and ourselves. Guys want the "hottest" girl and girls either want the "bad boy" or the "sweetheart." We are none of these things.

How far can looks get you in a relationship? That's lust, not love. Some hope that they can make that relationship work on looks. We are all very different from each other, but still very much the same. How we tell each other apart is through each other's eyes, and that is how we connect with that one love of life. You hope you see that look in someone else's eyes because that's when you know you have it.

Think about it...relationships don't start out with love. We hope they end up that way, but that is all it is...hope. We hope we fit in with a group, we hope we get good grades, we hope that the person we want more than anything wants us too. Friendships are made with hope. We hope that this person is somebody trustworthy and can be a true friend. We love them if they are, and we throw them away if they aren't. But we still hope. Hope is the most powerful thing in the world, because it will drive you to the ends of the universe and back again. Love can do that too, but hope carries more weight.

Everything we do is revolved around hope.

Hope is your prayer being answered and your wishes coming true. Hope is waking up next to the person of your dreams and knowing nothing will ever take that away. Hope is the couple that has been married for 55 years, but still can look at each other as if it were the first time that they ever saw each other. We hope we can have that. We hope that we are lucky enough to be that dream person or be that couple. We hope we can be successful like our heroes, we hope we can be as great as others around us. We hope that one day we have the privilege to see all the hard work pay off. We hope to be just like our moms and dads, or we hope to be the exact opposite of them. Love can't get you through life's worst obstacles. Having people that love you does help, but if you have no hope, then you have no chance of overcoming.

Hope is a feeling like no other. Hope alone won't get you the job you always desired, or the love of your life to randomly appear at that moment. But without hope, there is no chance of that happening. You don't think you will get that job, then you won't get that job. You have to hope that the job is yours, you have to hope that the person you've been waiting for is going to walk through those doors and have that same look in their eye. Hope is what you do when you want people to feel better. Hope is what you do when you want to make that team. Hope is what you want to become. That should be a life goal for people...to become someone else's hope.

Hope is knowing one day that that person will finally see what you have always seen in them. Hope is the last second shot to win a game, and the last pitch thrown to close out a win. Hope is everything from a newborn baby to an elderly woman who can't even remember her own name. We hope that baby stays healthy and lives a long life, and we hope that the elderly woman recovers. That is what humans do, we hope for each other.

Holding onto hope is our greatest challenge, because it is tested every day. Every bad grade, bad game, breakup, every bad event can lead to us losing hope. People find ways to cope with losing love, whether it be a night out or a pint of ice cream, there are coping mechanisms. Losing hope, however, isn't cured by ice cream or tears. Losing hope is only cured by finding something new to hope in. Hope is our dreams, our goals, and our ambitions. Hope is everything in this world. Love can be temporary, but we hope it lasts forever. The world runs on hope.

There are things that we can't control in life. We can't control events around us and we can't control love. We hold the key to our own destiny, because having hope is that key. Hope is that look in that other person's eyes that tells you this is it and this is the person I've been looking for. Love is so difficult because we never know where that look is, we never know where or who it will come from, and we never know when we missed our chance...until it's gone. That is why we strive for hope, not love.

Love can fade, but hope keeps us alive.

You Can Heal Your Life

In the infinity in life where i am, all is perfect, whole, and complete. Change is the natural law of my life. I welcome change. I am willing to change. I chose to change my thinking. I chose to change the words i use. I move from the old to the new with ease and with joy. It is easier for me to forgive then i thought. Forgiving makes me feel free and light. It is with joy that i learn to love myself more and more. The more resentment i release, the more love i have to express. Changing my thoughts makes me feel good. I am learning to choose to make today a pleasure to experience. All is well in my world.

Hello Person Reading this Letter

Yes, you. I'm speaking directly to you. I bet you had a hard day and would just like a warm blanket and a soft rub on your back.

I'm sorry I can't provide those things to you...but I am thinking really good, positive thoughts about you. I hope you are surrounded by love and that tomorrow you awaken to find something even better about your life.

Today, I ask you to take a deep breath and be thankful. I ask you to close your eyes and visualize a united world that is grateful for the little, perfect things around us every day. Have you seen a gerbera daisy? A stellar jay? Heard a baby's laughter?

Breathe deeply and thank whomever you can find. Thank them for the beautiful things that surround you. Thank them for your health. Thank them for your friends and family. Thank them for your home and your animals. Finally, thank them for your breath.

Do you feel it? It's called gratitude. It's free. It's in front of you. It's abundant. It only starts with a "thank you".

Thank you.

Thank a stranger tomorrow and mean it. Pass it on.

Love Is Your Choice

You would feel so much better if you would LET yourself care less about what others think about you, and just accept yourself. Let go of self-judgment and give yourself some much-needed love. If others are critical, accept it. Their opinions belong to THEM. In reality they do not determine a single thing about you. That is your choice! Know that you ARE beautiful, just as you are. When those negative thoughts pop into your head, accept them and let them pass. Don't judge yourself. Negative thinking builds up and it's like digging yourself into a hole. Positive thinking also builds up and if you get into the habit your love will begin to radiate, from deep in your heart, out to the surface, and into the universe, connecting with love that emanates from other people, animals, plants, earth, rocks, clouds, stars, everything you can imagine. You are surrounded by love 24/7!!!

Where has the laughter gone?

Happiness brings life... has everyone forgotten how to laugh and enjoy life? Take a deep breath people. Some days are stressful. Sometimes people hurt us or make us angry. Some things will just never make sense. And yet, we still all have the ability to choose how to deal with life. Find what brings you joy, and spend more time doing that one thing.

Laugh, people! Crack a joke, or even just a smile. Find a little humor in this crazy world... and GET HAPPY!

We just want to be loved. Is that so wrong?

That's what we are all searching for, hoping for — love.

It's so easy to accept it...but more difficult to give it.

Today, give it to the person who cuts you off on the freeway, give it to the lady who is short with you at the mall, give it to your boss who is driving you crazy, give it to the friend who has disappointed you.

Give the love. It's OK, you'll make more.

Let Love In

You may be thinking that you are hopeless in matters of love. And as the old saying goes, "Whether you think you can or you think you can't, you're right.

Open yourself up to love and it will find you.

I know that sounds hokey.

I know you are probably scribbling a nasty retort even as you're reading this telling me how wrong I am.

Hold on, there, put the pencil down...and just, for one moment,

Imagine if I'm right.

What would it hurt to try?

Head High

These may be the best of times. You may smile like you're holding the world in your hands. Or maybe you're plastering on a fake smile because the world is on your shoulders. Keep your head up. Watch your back. Smile at your friends, really smile. Read your enemies like you'd read a still snake. Take note of the gray clouds but also notice the life they bring below your feet. For every bad there's a good. And for every good, there's a fall. But don't let this fall cut you down forever. Get your ladder and climb out. Because life is short.

Peace and love.

on love

If I could heal your suffering, I would. If I could ease your pain, I would. Sometimes being helpless together makes it more bearable – so though I do not know you, I am with you. Though we have not spoken, I care about you. Though your story was not told, I listen and I cry.

I am sorry it takes so long to heal. There are just a few things we can truly learn in our short lives. One is that we can find meaning where we truly look, and especially in that which hurts the most. If you do not see it, be patient and loving with yourself. Look again, and then look again. You will find your meaning and your meaning will bear you up.

You are all people, you are unique in the universe, and you are beloved –

Peter

Something that needs saying

Dear everyone, everywhere:

Your worth as a human being isn't determined by your romantic status, or your waist size, or how tall you are. Nor is it dependent on your religion, your faith, or your diet of choice.

What it IS dependent upon is your ability to believe what you're worth. Which is, I gotta say, quite a lot. Don't underestimate your own capacity for being fucking awesome.

If you're ever feeling down or less than human, please just remember this: no matter who you are or what you look like, there is someone out there who loves you (you beautiful bastard) and that person is me.

Break free and own your life.

Much love,
someone

Be Extraordinary

Such a short time we spend on this planet.

So much wasted sitting and waiting for our lives to change.

We yearn for that ultimate sea change to put our lives on a different course but we don't know how to get on the boat. How do we make such a huge change? Why can't someone else decide our fate?

Well, who says change has to be huge? Or that a decision even has to be made?

Simply be extraordinary in a very small way. When you set to a task, put your stamp on it. When you serve dinner, set your plate in a beautiful manner; when you answer the phone, put on your best voice; when you hear a thank you, thank the other person greater...and mean it. Practice graciousness and pay it forward. Buy a stranger's coffee anonymously. Leave the change in the vending machine. Put your own art on the wall. Play kick the can with the neighborhood kids. Dress all in black and play ninja outside in the dark. Have a marshmallow roast in the winter. Hug your friends tightly and often.

Make a small effort (oh, is effort even the proper word?) and do one thing different and unexpected and see how you feel inside. If it feels right, try it again. If it feels wrong, try something else.

Live your unique life and soon you'll find yourself charting your own course.

Make it yours.

Peace to you.

hey you, you who look at yourself with imperfection

Guess what?

You're wrong to look at yourself that way.

You are more perfect than you know.

I look at you and the sun beams down upon your shoulders, when you smile-the light dances off those eyes. Those eyes that always look so sad.

I promise life will get better for you.

You deserve to be happy just as much as anyone else. Let love in and love with all you have. "Risk nothing, and chance losing everything."

So you have flaws...

Can I tell you a secret?

Everyone does. I was one of the most insecure people in the world until you looked right through me. You couldn't have made me feel so alive if you were as useless as you say. I love you.

Please smile more?

Your smile lights up my life...

Yes I'm Talking to You!

Dear everyone everywhere,

YOU ARE BEAUTIFUL. Every bit of you and even though I don't know you I know you are perfectly imperfect. You make mistakes and ask to be forgiven, hoping you won't be judged for your poor choices. You always try to put others before yourself. You do your best in school and work. You love those who are close to you and try and help them as best you can. You accept those who are different or people you aren't fond of and treat them with respect despite what they may have done to you. That is what makes a person beautiful. Not fancy clothes and tons of makeup, not popularity or how many times people compliment you. Beauty shines from the inside out. And you, yes YOU are beautiful.

Thanks for being you

and don't forget they might be right in front of you.

I love him forever; I want the world to know.

I want everyone to find love like this.

I want you all to know;

you are worth it...

you will find someone...

there is something special, out there for you to feel. it might not be today, tomorrow, or yesterday, you might have met a true keeper already, or you may not for a while. but love DOES exist, you CAN be happy. you can feel the song called love, and you will. everyone has someone. love will call you eventually. I wish you all luck, and hope, because you just might need something to tell you to hold on.

hold onto this; I know love, and I know how flighty it may feel, but you'll know it, it will come like a best friend you never knew you had.

please, don't let them define you

you're all fine.

just the way you are. with your mole, or your crooked teeth. with the curly hair that can't be tamed, and you with the bones so small you shop in the kid's section. you, who sees a flawed face in the mirror.

the one with the button nose, and the eyes set far apart. the one with a scar in her eyebrow.

you, with the curves in all the right places, or you with no curves at all,

you. are. beautiful.

no matter how you look, or who you are. if you are here, you're gorgeous to me.

Hold on to hope

To everyone out there,

There will be people out there who will hurt you. The people you love most in this world will hurt you. It's a part of what makes us human. But, the one amazing thing in this world that makes us human is our ability to hope. Never lose hope!! Always hold onto that little piece of hope no matter what...especially when it feels like you're encompassed in darkness. Let your hope light up the dark. Don't give up. Because things will get better.

HEY YOU!!! YES, YOU!!!!!

Hi. I don't know you and you don't know me.

But I love you... and you're beautiful/handsome and you should never let anyone bring you down.

You are worth so much and you are capable of anything, just never give up and never give in. It's not worth it.

The world is what it is and only by accepting it can we begin to change it. It is what we make it regardless of our past and present. It's your outlook and your decision which shapes the world around you!

So please, stay positive and remember that somewhere out there is someone that loves you and thinks you are amazing!! If God and our families can forgive us for our sins and mistakes why can't we forgive and except each other?!?!?!

Thank you dear LORD for the opportunity to be here on this day and see the beautiful world that you have trusted us with. We might not always appreciate it and act as we should but thank you for giving us chance after chance to make a change!

Hopefully one day we as the human race will be able to show you how much we appreciate it!

AMEN

Dream Big.

Our day to day lives are filled with such minutiae and we give it so much importance. Yes, paying bills are important and having food in the house is necessary and making sure your children are clean is essential.

But what about you? What have you done for you lately?

Take a moment. Just stop. Stop everything. Close your eyes. Take a deep breath. Listen to the world around you. Hear the birds or the wind rustling through the trees. Be in the moment.

Now ask yourself, 'What do I want?'

Dream big. Dream honestly. What do you want?

The old adage is that the journey of a thousand miles begins with one step. It doesn't have to be a big step to put you on your way to your dreams...but it does have to be a step.

So make it a small one. Just make it.

Big dreams with small steps. In time, I promise you'll get there.

Silence

Dear you,

I hope you find happiness. I hope you find peace. I hope you find someone who cares about you as much as I do. I want you to know that I'll always keep you around in my thoughts. Things will look up, I promise. There are going to be points in your life that seem like they can't get any better any time soon, but soon. Soon they'll get better. You can always assume the worst and hope for the best, but sometimes you shouldn't assume the worst. You may be cynical but you need to work on that, try to forget about things happening. Live life for the moment, and stop expecting the worst to happen, stop planning for things that will never happen. You're worth something to someone; you just need to find them. I know you hate the silence; you need to find something to fill the silence. It'll get better from here, don't worry.

Hope

For all of you out there that are hurting yourselves, cutting yourselves, starving yourselves, hating yourselves, wanting to kill yourselves...please don't...there are people that you don't even know that love you and can help you.

It makes me so sad reading all of your posts.

If you are reading this right now...know that there is hope. Even if you don't believe it...there is.

I was there once and now I am free from depression, suicidal thoughts, hopelessness.

Reach out please and pray to God! Even if you don't believe there is one! Just do it as an experiment and see what happens...I did and I am now free. Just say "Please God help me! I'm hurting and I can't do this! I can't live this life by myself! I need your help! Ask and you shall receive!

Believe me, I am living proof. There is hope:)

You're Not Reading This By Accident

This is meant for you.

I wish you love. I wish you joy. I wish you happiness.

May you wake every morning looking forward to your day and put your head down every evening tired and satisfied.

Your life is too short to wonder what could have been. Instead, wonder, 'What next?'

Be kind to the people around you and love them even when they make you mad.

Tip your servers and help them to have a better day.

Be gracious to the elderly.

Spread love.

Peace.

this isn't made for a dead end

stop hesitating.
jump in.
ask her out.
kiss him hard.
say I love you, because they might be gone tomorrow.
hug your parents, even if you are fighting.
go adopt a shelter animal.
call an old friend.
look in the mirror and point out the things you love, instead of picking
at things you hate.
tell a friend a secret that's bursting inside you.
do.
live.
you're beautiful.
feel that way.

if you need a pick me up,

Dear those reading this letter, and many others, and those who are writing letters too.

I want to inspire, I want to make you smile. I want to think of something raw and beautiful to show life to those who can only see dark and pain.

I don't know what words to say, I want to act upon these thoughts in my daily life, and make just one person feel meaningful. Because you are. We all are, whatever God we believe in or don't, whatever gender, sexuality, whatever weight and eye color.

I want to make everyone see, that there is more than meets the eye in this life, and we can all make someone feel significant.

life.

Okay.

So many of you, living people, go through the day without taking a second look at things. Let me evaluate a bit on what you are doing. I know that I don't have the power to change anything about your perspective but I can try, can't I?

Well, listen or read closely.

Gandhi once said that whatever you do in life will be insignificant but it's very important that you do it, because nobody else will.

Live by this, and I promise you you'll have the power to overcome even your own objections.

You have a strong heart and you are capable of loving and caring and LIVING.

Don't doubt your inner self.

I don't know who you are but I love you, even if the world hates you, you are wrong, because here I am telling you I love you.

Be the person you want to be, don't copy anyone else, don't die as a copy – die as an original.

Don't believe in god. You don't have to, to be strong in the mind. Follow what your heart feels like you should. And forever does have an ending to it, but it also has to have beginnings.

Do you matter?

This goes deeper than whether you matter to the guy you've been mooning over or the parent who left your family, the friend who talked smack about you or the girl you've been trying to impress.

Do YOU matter?
Do you matter to the person who you just cut off on the freeway?
Do you matter to the old lady you helped park her car?
Do you matter to the waiter that you blatantly ignored when they followed up on your meal?
Do you matter to the telemarketer you just swore at?
Do you matter to the person receiving your donated blood?
Do you matter to the stranger on the street you just smiled at?
Do you matter to the teacher that you wrote to thank them for making a positive influence on your life?
Do you matter to the neighbor when you, without asking, mowed their lawn?
Do you matter to the next person who really needs that extra penny?
Do you matter to the person you just made fun of in front of others?
Do you matter to the person you just held while they cried?
Do you matter to the person you just made laugh?
Yes.
We all, each of us, matter. Everything we do matters.
But HOW do we matter?
Do we matter as a positive that might change another's day for the better or do we matter as a negative that might alter another's life for the worse?

Each action, be it positive or negative, is but a drop in the ocean of our world-wide collective but that single drop forms a ripple that spreads farther than we can see.

Each drop matters more than we can imagine.

So today, matter for the better.

hopefully...

I want to make the world happy, I want to tell any person out there with no hope for love, with no hope for anything in their life,

there is a reason to live!
love does exist!
everyone is beautiful!

Everything is worth living for; just look outside your window, that world is not worth seeing? your future is not worth anything? how can you know? what if in two days, someone was going to ask you out? or if in a week, someone was going to tell you that they think you are an amazing person?

I think you are an amazing person. I think you are beautiful.

someone, somewhere needs to hear how amazing they are. those who have hope...go tell them! go smile at a stranger and hug your best friend, give your mom a handmade card and help your dad clean up the yard.

simple things, life is too short to give up before you have seen it.

I love you.

A letter for the lonely

To everyone I see with a broken heart,

Know that you are not alone. You are beautiful, you are handsome, you are smart, you are funny. You will become something amazing as long as you don't give up. Say goodbye to the cheaters, the beaters, the liars, and the thieves. You deserve someone as amazing as you are and don't let anyone tell you differently. If anyone has broken your heart believe in Karma. Good or bad what goes around comes around and there is something amazing waiting for you. Love yourself before you love another.

Sincerely,
The one who bears a broken heart on her sleeve.

Stop asking permission

I have to admit that my advice is born from learning this the hard way. I met a woman. A smart, beautiful woman. We clicked in a way I've never clicked with anyone, she knew me better than people I've known for years and I 'got' her better than I've ever gotten anyone.

Trouble was, though it wasn't exactly forbidden, the trouble either of us would have had to go through to actually make a relationship happen was more than either of us were willing to go through. It's like we were both waiting for someone to give us permission to feel the things we were already feeling very strongly.

Not taking that chance I'll admit has not ruined my life. In fact I'm with a nicer caring person than her, even if there is little of the clear almost 'magical' ability to communicate we had betwixt the two of us, I've met someone who is willing to fight for me. Someone who is not just willing to passively accept what is going on, but actively attempt to change what is for the better.

So the point is, stop waiting for someone to tell you it's ok. Now I'm not advising anyone to break the law or invade someone's space, but our society is far too polite. We often care a little bit too much about what people will think and say rather than how we'll feel if we never take that chance. Know when to admit defeat, but as far as you can, pursue what you love and makes you happy. No one's going to deliver it to you on a silver platter, but thankfully we are powerful enough to chart our own destiny.

It may seem foolish and ill advised, but it beats wondering what would have happened if you'd gone out on a limb, sure you could end up embarrassed, but if you never risk anything chances are you're never going to gain anything either.

Peace and happiness to you,

Orestes

Today

Is the day, tell him you love him, call her up and ask her to dinner. Fuck what everyone else thinks, it's YOU who will need to be happy in the end.

Don't just stand there with your mouth open wide, go fucking do it! Take the plunge, chances are they feel the same too.

And if they don't, oh well, you should feel proud you took control in your life.

Life is too damn short to hesitate and worry yourself. Just make a choice.

Trust me.

Life

I believe that things happen for a reason. People come in and out of your life, you choose who stays. There is more good in life than bad, take the time to see the good. Happiness is a way of life and it's the cure to all pain. When you feel something for someone or have something you're dying to say, say it. Think of life in a way that there might not be the chance to say what you wanted to say tomorrow. You should say what you feel. You don't want to live with regret for not expressing your feelings.

Life is full of obstacles and one day you will realize that you need to wake up and take the challenge. The only regret one should have in life is not saying something they needed to say. You go through life with all these different emotions. The things you do happen, you shouldn't regret something you did but regret something you didn't say. In a way that may not make sense. Look at it this way, you can't take back something you did. You can speak your mind and express yourself because that is the true meaning of why we all live. To go through life experiencing different things. Learn to love and learn to live.

I fell in love and I'm still in love. I go through life being a hypocrite. I think more about the bad than the good. It's not a good way to live life. It not only affects you, it affects everyone around you. Even those that are most important to you. I feel more pain than anyone should. It's not something anyone should feel sorry for me about. I have been through terrible things in my life. Things no one should ever have to go through. But it happens and there's nothing you can do to change the past. Just learn to let go, love those closest to you. Try your best to never let go. Love with all your heart. Try to be happy.

Love, Me

When the world stops turning

What the world really needs to realise is that we are all nothing but monkeys. We are relatively smart upright walking monkeys... We are biological in nature, and therefore are no more important to the universe than the ferns. We die and disappear forever... So if you read this – please believe me when i say you only live ONCE. You are alive ONE time. You will not get a second chance to come back and say all those things you wanted, do all those things you longed for. Tell that man/woman you LOVE THEM. Dance in public! You are fucking SEXY. The world is full of a lot of other silly upright walking monkeys... don't act like you're different because you're not. We're allllll the same. And we're allllll going to die. Make yourselves happy and say what's in your heart.

Let's be brave!

I read so many messages on here about people being scared to tell someone how they feel. (I, too, am guilty of writing a few of those...) But what if, collectively, we all gathered the courage to ACTUALLY tell said person, and finally let ourselves breathe, if only for a second.

If they like us back, things will be fine. If they don't; our hearts can break, and we can finally move on to find the next wonderful person.

I dare you to be brave. And I will be too.

In the Light!!

Life is only confusing because we have a natural tendency to make it that way. We have desires, wants, expectations and when reality doesn't coincide with all these we feel stressed, confused, tired, and maybe even lost at what to do and where to turn. But life, if you really look at it, is kinda simple.

These things that we want (a certain type of job, car, wealth, etc.) are not things that we need. Without them we are still the same person, and yet, we toil for and worry about all these things day after day. That's where life gets confusing. If we just focused on what we actually needed to be happy (food, shelter, family, love), and didn't let other's opinions/views have so much hold over us, maybe life would be a little simpler for us all?

I guess it really comes down to how one wants to live their life, what makes them happy, and how they want to be seen by others (if they even care about that).

I'm sure there are times when everything just seems to fall away, when all our "responsibilities" seem to disappear and we are 100% happy, everything appears small and insignificant then, right? Those are the times when we realize (like when looking at the stars) that maybe everything we're after isn't all we thought it to be, maybe we realize that these things will come our way if they are meant to, maybe it's here that we finally release a little bit of control and pick up a little more faith...

Live.

The world begins to pale. Ever so slightly.

As if it were trying to slip away unnoticed.

You are far too beautiful to leave without a bang.

Stand out. You are stunning. And different. Appreciate others for the talent they have and don't be envious.

You have so much already.

You are you.

Meet yourself.

You're amazing.

A Chain Letter of Love

This will not make you rich, thin, smart or successful...unless you consider the richness in your heart, the thinning of your hatred and the smart look on your face as you become successful in love.

Be kind to somebody today. Take that extra step to open a door, hand over a dollar — whether that be a street person or someone short at a cashier, hug a friend extra tight, call your mother — not because you need money, laundry, comfort...but just because you love her, send your sister or brother a "thinking of you" card. Just do SOMETHING. Put a little more love out there. Encourage the same.

Put out a chain letter of love...because Love is the only thing that gets greater when given away.

Oh, and absolutely nothing bad will happen if you don't. YOU are still loved.

my plea.

we sit in our warm homes on cold nights, and eat meals after a long day, and wake up and do the same. yet we do not stop to think about those who do not have the same pleasures.

we are all so fragile. so young, despite our chronological age. we need each other. we need love. we need to help those who are literally drying on the streets. or so lonely they wish they were dying. we are all together. we should all act together.

do not hate. do not use mean words. forgive quickly because life has so much more. we can all give so much more. this is my plea. my final thoughts. we all need you.

The (Not So) Big Picture

Hello.

When you really think about it, the scientific process of life is astounding and miraculous. And so often are we surrounded by it that we sometimes forget how beautiful it is. I'm not telling you to cry the next time you see a sunset or pick the first flower you see. But think: life is so quick. We are so insignificant. It's in the general population's best interest to make their life goal to have a positive and significant impact on the world, whatever it may be. Life's too short to be angry, because when you die, people will eventually forget you. Or will they? It's up to you.

Yep.

Friend,

Do me a favor, please.

Be passionate. Okay? Be passionately well. Make yourself the very best thing that you ever wanted to be. Be the kind of person you've always wanted to be. Take risks. Belly-laugh all deep and throaty and cry when you do. If you want to be a little sad, if you want to be destructive, make it count. Make it gorgeous. Don't waste a moment of who you are. Don't be half-hearted. Run down the sidewalk. Jaywalk. Don't be careful. Don't let yourself be jaded. Don't let yourself fold over into complacency. Don't give up. Love someone. Get ready for me.

(I'll be doing the same.)
I'm so excited to meet you one day.

Day one.

Step one. Breathe.

Step two. Remember to breathe again.

Step three. Stay away from railroad tracks, knives, and passing cars.

"I as I, and not as we."

Dear Whoever Reads This

No matter what anyone, no matter whom, has said or done to you in the past, you are beautiful. You have gotten up after being hit, whether physically or emotionally, and for that I applaud you. Something as simple as your smile brings joy into stranger's lives. Keep doing what you're doing, and someone out there, someone like me, will keep appreciating you. Always smile big, laugh loud, spread love. Lord knows there aren't enough people in the world doing it. You are one of those rare people who make the world a better place by simply existing.

This is to those people who wake up in the morning, and their first thought is not about what they have to do today, or what happened to them yesterday, or what's going on tomorrow. From the moment they awake they are worried about how to make the world a better place for you, for me, to live in.

These people never get the recognition they need.

Thank you for making the world a better place

I'll always love you, regardless of anything at all. You are beautiful inside and out.

You're doing something right.

You deserve it!

I don't want you to be sad.

To everyone who wants a lover, a person they can turn to whenever they need them, I hope and pray you find them soon. I hope you find the person you fit with like a puzzle piece; you'll know when you meet them.

I hope for every one broken heart I have read on this site, I hope someone finds stitches and puts you back together.

I hope for every tortured, anguished person on here, who can't make a decision I hope it comes to you in a small moment in your day and everything falls into place again.

For every betrayed friend on here, don't forget YOU ARE AMAZING, you don't deserve to be treated like crap, you are a wonderful person.

For ANYONE on here who is upset, and needs something, I hope you get what you need, and know that all of us here, we're listening, we'll talk to you, you are loved.

Strangers, but friends, I wish nothing more but for your utter happiness.

live it

Today's a new day. Forget about yesterday. Don't worry about tomorrow. Go out and live your life.

Have fun. Live it up. Do your thing. It'll be over before you know it.

Oh, and call your mother. She misses you.

To everyone who feels unloved forgotten feels like it doesn't matter or has been through hell

This is for YOU.
Yes YOU and only YOU.
Life sucks. It's hard.
You're going through things.
You're confused angry and hurt.
You feel like nobody listens.
Nobody cares, nobody's there.
Sometimes you wonder if it's worth it.
If you really matter
If anybody would notice if you ended it.
You feel controlled.
You rebel. You don't care.
You wish somebody would understand.
You plaster a smile on your face just to please.
You go on with your day
and you pretend everything is fine.
You're scared you want help
but you can't reach out.
Just know that you are loved.
Someone out there in this world cares.
Someone in this world knows your value.
It doesn't matter if I know your name
It doesn't matter if i know your story
It doesn't matter what you're going through
will go through or what you've done.
My heart goes out to you
I feel for you. I care.
I accept you for who you are.
I wish that I could know you.
I'm here. Not physically but emotionally and mentally.
I understand maybe not completely but in other ways.
So please hang in there you're not alone.

Please fight because you're worth it
even though it doesn't seem like it.
Please try. Look within yourself
you have what it takes to make it through
whatever life throws your way.
And don't let people judge you
unless they've lived in your shoes
they have no right or reason to.
And when you feel like life's too much
look at the sky and remember me.
I care and I'm here and I always will be.

dear reader

dear reader, i don't have much to say. I decided to write simply to remind you that this world is beautiful.

I know what it is like to be abused, to be mistreated, to spend each day in depression, but nothing would ever stop me from seeing the beauty in this world, you can see it too.

close your eyes, i will hold your hand, and tell you that this world is beautiful, you make it beautiful, so don't give up, you are needed and loved from a stranger far away who still chose to believe in the beauty of this world.

To You, Reading This, Right Now

The very fact that you care enough about other people to actually read through the issues of people you've never met tells me you are a good person.

I want to tell you, no matter how badly life is going for you right now, it gets better.

And no matter how good it's going right now... it gets even better than this.

So, lovely, beautiful person reading this, stand tall and stay strong. You've got someone rooting for you, even if you don't know who they are. You matter to people, and even if it's just one person, that means you are making an active difference on this earth. You are important to someone, you are loved by many someones-and that group of someones should include yourself. Because, let's face it, you're awesome.

—Bb

Perceptions

This message is addressed to anyone who is listening; anyone who is too afraid to be who they are, anyone who is smiling on the outside but hurt on the inside, anyone who thinks that they aren't better than anyone else. This letter is for the girls who were constantly reinforced that looks are the only thing that matter in the world, who constantly look for a dangerous relationship because they believe that they can 'save' someone. This is also addressed to the guys who think that no matter what they do that they won't amount to anything just because some girl who is your best friend won't ever see you in a romantic way, because you weren't the strongest kid in the weight room, because you were too busy studying rather than getting drunk in high school.

I don't know what everyone has been telling you. I don't know how the world has gotten the way it has, but that's not what I am here to tell you. I am here to say that you are unique. You are special. You are made to be who you want to be and no one should stop you. You are beautiful, regardless of weight or ethnic background, even if your peers are too self-centered to know that beauty is on the inside. You can't save those who don't want to be saved and you should never be someone else's punching bag, whether the punching is done mentally or physically. Causing yourself pain (be it by staying in an unstable relationship or by cutting yourself) is never an answer; it's not fair to yourself. Stability cannot be found in an unstable environment, don't keep searching for it there.

To those of you who are suicidal, those of who you believe that no one can understand your pain and that you are lonely in the world, have faith. Talk. I can guarantee you that while people may not be able to relate to you, there will be at least one person who will be willing to sit down and talk to you, even if that person is a complete stranger at a nursing home.

To those of you who have made mistakes, no one is judging you. If you want to make up for whatever you have done, people will listen. They may not respond positively, but they will hear you. That's all you can do in those situations.

And to those of you who feel unloved, there is always something that loves you, even if it is only a cat or a dog. They are often the only thing that will not abandon you in tough times.

I love you. I believe in you. I trust you. I need you. I think you're beautiful, but most of all, I believe that you are irreplaceable.

This Is Meant For You.

You file through these letters, hoping maybe a surprise lays in wait. A gem, waiting for you, beyond all the tales of hidden loves and untold fantasies.

Well, this is for you. This is me telling you that no matter who you are, no matter where you're from, you are brilliant. You have been the source of more smiles and laughter than you could ever begin to imagine. You have been the light of someone's life for longer than you could think. Out there someone cares about you more than you will ever be able to know.

So keep that with you. Know that to someone you are a unique model who no-one will ever be able to replace. You will always have a space reserved in their heart.

So in the end, everyone has a love letter waiting.

YOU.

You. Yes, you. I am writing this for you.

I know you are reading this. And I want you to know I am writing this for you. No one else will understand. No one else knows. They think that this is for them. But it's not. I am writing this for you.

I want you to know, life...it's hard. Every day can be a challenge. It can be a challenge to get up in the morning. To get yourself out of bed. To put on that smile. But I want you to know, that smile is what keeps me going some days. You need to remember, even through the tough times, you are amazing. You really are.

You should be happy. You are gorgeous.

I know that the weather might not be perfect. You might have to turn your back to the wind or feel the cold nipping at your nose. But you know what; at least you are there to feel it. At least you can enjoy the sun's warm rays on your face. Or that cold February wind biting at your cheeks. You know what that means?

You are alive.

Everything will be okay.

dear freaks

This goes out to all the unwritten songs rotting in paralyzed hands of whom society calls freaks. The silent ones with unique clothes, catching second glances of confused eyes that look back a third time with disgust of the difference. The artists who dare to spare pride for meaningful pieces which reveal themselves while pointing fingers critique the paint-stained people who don't point back but simply keep creating. Quirky Bob Dylan types with your long greasy hair and skinny jeans. This is for you. You are so beautiful, a masterpiece, greater than all of yours combined. Thank you so much for being you and not being afraid to step across the line with your paintbrush, cigarette stained breath, grungy clothes, black eyeliner, or that old guitar your grandpa gave you. Thank you for being people who inspire and wear your peace signs around your neck, right next to that heart so proudly shown on your sleeve. Keep being you, because without you the world would be black and white with no color, silent with no music, and boring with no strange clothes and interesting hairdos. I can't wait to see you come up with next.

Sky.

Life.

I look around the lobby of my school. All these souls, these people. What are they doing?

Learning, living, we're all going through something. As I dive beneath the layers of those who open up to me. I've never been alone. We've all been hurting. The daily struggles that everyone goes through.

Every night I stare up at the stars, and realize just how small I am, and just how meaningless everything is. But...then I realize just how beautiful it is.

That maybe, we are just all here by chance. That maybe the meaning of life isn't the destination. Maybe it's the journey. Maybe we have to find meaning; make our own meaning. Maybe every day that you get hurt, is a day that you get stronger. You've probably heard this so much haven't you? Life is beautiful. The pain, the sadness...is beautiful.

I'm alive.

You're alive.

And you'll make it through this. No matter how hard it gets.

The lights above will never fade, as long as you keep looking up.

Good-night.

Pillars of Support

I honestly don't understand the need for one's own self in a life. I believe we are more motivated to make other people's lives better than our own. That leads to people seeing others to their true potential, even if that person doesn't. Because other people are motivated to help others, that leads to bigger success and more happiness in the person's life. I truly believe, and I have experienced this through my own life, that helping others reach their potential, not only makes them happy, but makes me feel like I've actually done something with my life. Not just sat around trying to get to the top. I'd rather be the pillar holding up the building, than the building itself. No one notices any individual pillar, and nor should anyone notice just one person. But what the pillars represent is the power of human cooperation for the betterment of another thing that is not their own. Pillars don't do anything except help something else support itself. That's what we need. We need to be pillars for others; we need to support other people. Because in supporting others we find that we support ourselves.

You.

To you.

Yes, I'm talking to you, not anyone else, just you reading because this letter was written for your sake. I know it's hard and I know what you're thinking. But it's ok because every time you wake up in the morning and force yourself out of bed and put on that same smile, you are someone people look up to. Maybe not even people you know but they are there and they admire you when you aren't looking.

Life might seem cold and sometimes the winter wind may bite at your nose and the wind may howl at your back but be glad that you are here at all to experience that because you are truly beautiful. and I mean that- just you this is meant for you.

You are absolutely beautiful. Stunning. Amazing.

And don't let anyone ever tell you differently. There are people out there that admire people like you and there are people who thrive on your smile.

Please don't give up. It's people like you that are the most beautiful people of all.

You're Beautiful

Anyone and everyone-

no matter where you've been, where you're going, or what you've done, it's never too late to be who you want to be. don't let anyone tell you, you are not good enough to accomplish a dream you have. i don't know you personally, but i believe in you. no matter what anyone says, you are beautiful. take this to heart because i'm sending it straight from mine. be yourself, and be brave and take risks. today is never too late to be brand new. trust me people, i know what i'm talking about. you are loved, whether you believe it or not.

-Darcy

Everything

This letter is not directed to one specific person but humanity as a whole.

I don't know why bad things happen in life but I do know that at the end of the day, our hardships make us stronger. It gives us our experience and develops our morals.

I think we need more love in our country though. Because after all, we live on the same planet so therefore we are family. No matter what race, gender, sexuality or social class. Family does not abandon each other in a time of need. Every day we should be striving to help somebody or go out of our way to smile at a stranger on the street because you never know what they are going through.

Life is life and we need to make the best of it even during the thick and thin. And this might sound cliché and you may have heard it said in anonymous letters like this but you are loved. That's the truth.

Much Love,
Me.

Courage

"Courage is not the towering oak that sees storms come and go, it is the fragile blossom that opens in the snow." Alice M. Swaim

And since most of us are not towering oaks for the most part, but mere fragile blossoms at heart, we recognize courage as the daily daring to express ourselves with evermore gentle vulnerability and ever less callous indifference if we are to continue enjoying the sunlight.

Be Confident

Dear girl who is still searching,

You are beautiful. In and out. You are on your way to becoming someone great and no one can block your path. You need to stop listening to the boys around you that are trying to tear you down. Stop trying to live someone else's life. Start feeling comfortable in your own skin. Tell the world "this is me, and if you don't like it, tough". It's going to be hard at first, but it is worth it.

Stop giving in to others and start doing what you want to do. Stop drinking. It only leads to more mistakes and can bring you no closer to your goals. The boys that want to kiss you when you're drunk and take you home are not the boys you want to be with. You deserve someone much better.

You deserve someone who is going to be with you through it all. You deserve someone who loves you for who you are. You deserve someone who is going kiss you good morning, someone who is going to massage your feet after a long day, someone who is going to be yours forever. You deserve your prince charming. Wait for him. He will come.

Dear You,

Whenever you feel alone in the world, just take a look around you. You are surrounded by love. There is evidence of it everywhere, from the numerous "Thinking of You" greeting cards scattered about your desk, to the pictures of your smiling little cousins taped to your wall, to the many people who greet you with a big grin and an even bigger embrace.

And you deserve all of this love. Never let yourself believe that you don't. You're smart, talented, passionate, and have a heart that is almost too big for your tiny body. You are beautiful. Even on the days when you feel disgusting, you are beautiful. Just remember this- no one cares about your muffin top or the huge zit on your chin. No one, that is, except for yourself.

So, don't stress yourself out too much. Remember that "perfection" is nothing but a myth. Do things for the sole reason that you enjoy doing them. Eat chocolate, drink wine. Do yoga, read Cosmo. Sing. Write poetry, and color just to feel like a kid again. For now, just focus on making yourself happy. In time, someone will enter your life and you will finally feel complete. Just know that before you even begin to love another person, you have to love yourself.

Love, Me

Dear You,

You're beautiful. I know the world gets cold and lonely and miserable, but please, just know that no matter what, there will be someone who cares about you and loves you. Never hurt yourself, because in hurting yourself, you're hurting those around you, too. Even when things seem like they're as bad as they can get, there will always be something to live for and some reason to be strong. I love you. I may not know you. I may never have met you and I may never see you in my life, but I love you and I care about you. Please, never forget. There are people who care. Always.

Love, me

STOP and read.

Listen. Just listen. Well, I guess... read.

Each one of you here, you have a purpose. I have a purpose. Even if it's as minute as being a reader on this site, you are providing a community, and an outlet, for all of us here that need one in the worst way. You are a part of something; it's something that's incredibly powerful and a necessary part of so many of our lives. Everyone that reads this has been a part of something wonderful, and an integral part in my being here right now.

So thank you. Each and every one of you that reads this is providing for me a form of expression, one that if I was without, I'm not sure I'd still be here. You are so important to me. And the fact that YOU mean this much to me, and I haven't met any of you... it's just incredible how much you must mean to those you come in contact with every day. Keep doing what you do; keep giving all of us this outlet; and keep touching everyone you come into contact with, because you never know how much your small action, like coming to read this letter, can mean to those around you. Thank you, I needed it.

Opened Eyes

I feel overwhelmed with letters based on relationship issues; it's an immense realisation of how much the love/hate spectrum has such an impact on our empathetic communicational desires; for reassurance, answers and hope.

These extreme feelings of love, hate and fear drive our body to behave in abnormal ways we cannot explain or control... because at the end of the day, it's those emotions alongside the rest that control us!

Your life is a cyclopean improbability which has ended in you, against all the odds you're the result of an incredible process of nature. It's this which guarantees most of us a soul mate.

You may be young, you may be old, but the bottom line is that the majority of your stress shouldn't be down to heart break. Everyone goes through a tough time in their life which causes a large amount of frustration and depression, yet what's the one thing everyone has in common? Well once time is taken out of the equation everyone gets over it. Life is too short to waste your youthful and productive time on letting the problems you encounter take its toll. The only thing you're allowing to happen is an unwanted suffering.

Life is for you to do the things you want to do. Most ask why they cannot do the things they want to do even they know what which is silly : the trick is that you're always doing what you want to do, no one's making you do anything. Once understood you realise you're free and realise that life has always been free will pushing towards or away from a purpose.

Don't cave in – you're always as strong as you need to be... Wake Up!

It's short.

Life's short, everyone says "simplify your life." Yeah right, like that's gonna happen, that's something i would read in one of those stupid home and garden magazines. Life is so damn complicated that it isn't even funny. So here is MY personal list of how life should be lived. This is for all the people who think they have the right to tell you how to live. This is to your "friends", your boss, your parents, your class mates, your teachers, the public, the media, the government, heck, this is for the whole damn world.

1. Make life hectic; see how much you can take till you explode.
2. Love so much more than your heart can hold, because all that really matters is wonderful, passionate love and death.
3. Eat the most delicious food you can get a hold of, who cares if you put on 5 more pounds, you shouldn't care! If you're trying to impress someone with your body then they aren't worth the time.
4. Everyone is full to the brim with bull shit, you are the only one who can make the rules to your world, all of the rules that other people make up are only suggestions.
5. Don't sleep more than you have to, you're missing out on all the fun.
6. Why are you still reading this? I told that everyone is full of shit, that includes me! Don't take my advice, go make some mistakes out there in the world and get your lazy ass of the computer.

Afterword

Originally, when I started this letter, it came out so negative. I dug up feelings from a long time ago and spread them out on this page with the hope that after it was done and posted, I'd feel better about what happened. But really, once I finished what I had to say, I already felt better.

So I erased it. Now, I'm writing to a different end.

This is for all of you out there. All of the writers and all of the readers. I just want to say that you could be reading a letter of earnest hate. There could be curse words, anecdotes, loathing incarnate in this passage. But there isn't. I want to present something positive, something warm.

I know there are times when things feel absolutely awful. Your heart feels like it's in a vice, and someone you care about it intentionally pressing down on the handle. You feel like all the controls are being wrenched away from you, that no matter how you try, you'll never get back on your feet. It can be a hopeless, maddening place, and at one time or another I imagine many of us have been there.

Don't give up. You can make it. I bet all of you have heard this a million times before, and I bet there are plenty of letters on this site dedicated to it. But it bears repeating. Never give up. Things do improve, and one day you'll be sitting where I am. You'll be in a position where even when you try and muster all of your anger or sadness, you find that halfway through, it doesn't even bother you anymore.

And when you get there, maybe you'll feel like writing a letter too.

Things I wish I could say

You are going through a tough time, and I'm sorry. I wish I could help you through this. I want you to know you are a wonderful person with a wonderful soul. Life has given you a different path than the one you thought you would take. Difficulties are beginning to show, but you can do it on your own. I believe that good people are rewarded at some point, that point just isn't in view yet. Never think that you are anything less than wonderful. Good people are hard to find in this world, so please don't lose that as you go along this winding road. I love you as a friend, and I hope you understand that I will be three steps behind you... watching you succeed and pushing you when you feel the climb is too high.

So Live.

Now. Think A Moment.

It's hard. Deal.

It's painful. So what?

It's difficult. Get over it.

Life isn't meant to be cut and dry. Black and white. Sweet or salty. If it were easy you'd be bored. So love wildly. Work diligently. Play often. You've heard it before. Hear it again. Remind yourself. I'm alive. Every day. You're one of the lucky ones. Revel in it. Cry. Hurt. Move on. Stop complaining. We've all been there. We're all human. Don't forget that. Ever.

It's hard? Good.

It's painful? So smile.

It's difficult? That is life.

Now. Go Live It.

You. Right there.

yes, you. You are a beautiful.

These times might be hard, but you just have to live. Live for tomorrow. Live for the next day, which brings new people, new experiences.

Right now you may feel down on love or luck, and things may seem hopeless, but right now. right now.

You are wondering if you'll ever find that one person.

The one person who you'll wake up next to every morning for the rest of your life. Who you will share your most deepest feelings and secrets and desires with. Who will love you no matter what you look like, or are wearing, or are even saying or thinking.

And if you weren't, you are now.

Well that person? That person is wandering the earth RIGHT NOW, and is thinking the same think as you are. Keep going for that soul. For that other half of yourself that you haven't even met yet.

Because chances are, they're doing the same for you.

Right now may seem like everything is hopeless, delicate, and vulnerable. You may not want to accept something in fear you may be hurt in the process.

But when push comes to shove, it's a life lesson. And that pain proves you're living and alive and having new experiences. That pain, you will be able to wear like a medal and in due time, you will be able to say that you are proud of yourself for pushing through such a tough time in your life. In the grand scheme of things, this is only one year out of your life.

One. Year.

Out of 86, give or take a few.

So why not? Why not live and take those chances? Because when you're sitting in that rocking chair, looking over your grandchildren, there is no doubt that you will regret not doing what you know deep down inside.

Push through this. I know you can.

A Few Facts Of Life

You are beautiful, inside and out. Don't let anyone tell you otherwise. Anyone who does is jealous.

You are you. Don't let anyone change that. The people who matter are the people who will accept and love you for who you are, not who you pretend to be.

Respect yourself. If you respect yourself, others will respect you. People don't respect you for being intimidating; they respect you for being a strong person.

Never give up. Life is full of obstacles and hard times, but it's those hardships that make you a stronger person. And without sadness, happiness wouldn't be nearly as special.

Enjoy the small moments of happiness in life. Life may be full of hardships, but it's also full of happy moments that most people tend to overlook. If you can't learn to enjoy those moments, you will be bitter for the rest of your life.

Smile. Smiling is good for your health. Really.

These are just a few things that everyone should keep in mind. Don't lose hope. Know that there's always someone out there who cares even when you feel like you're completely alone. <3

Just Sometimes.

Just sometimes. I have the impulse to stand outside and just stare upwards, stare into space for a while until everything about me becomes a sea of calm.

Just sometimes. I like to walk, for no reason, in any direction. Slow walks heading to somewhere new, somewhere i can experience new sights, sounds and smells. A place where exploring isn't something old.

Just sometimes. I sit down with a pen and paper and make my imagination come to life, scrawl down all the random thoughts i have and make a vast story of craziness, just because i can.

Just sometimes. I'll sing in the middle of the night, sing songs of happiness with lyrics of joy.

I don't do these things because I'm insane.

I do them because life isn't about complaining about details, it's about enjoying those details, life is for living.

So live it.

A Graduation Speech, that I never spoke

Be Reckless.

If I had any words of advice to give, these two strike me as the most important.

Be reckless, because twenty years from now you will look back and be more disappointed by the things you didn't do rather than the things you did.

Don't worry. People judge a man's character by their stride and not their stumble. There is no time for fear, but plenty for foolishness.

Stay passionate. Life comes at you in a myriad of colors. A masterpiece is not painted with an artist's eyes closed.

Keep dancing, even if there is no music, even if it is raining, even if everyone is watching and you don't know the steps. Forget the steps. Life is more fun when you make it up as you go.

Get Lost.

Find Yourself.

Time Passes, such truths we hold to be inevitable, but do not plan a second of it, for time passes too quickly to worry.

Grow old. Wisdom comes with years.

Stay young, and do fall often. There is always room for falling. Fall while balancing books on your head or when you spin in circles with your arms outstretched. Fall down and scrape your knees. Fall after trying to reach that last jar on the shelf.

Fall in love. Because this solitary emotion, although clumsy and dizzy, can make worthwhile every day. Always remember, without it, your life is wasted.

Hate is apparent, but seldom should it be reflected in your day. There will be some things you just can't stand from large injustices to one-ply toilet paper. Never let it keep you from succeeding. Give your opponent a chance to explain. Give them time so you can understand.

Forgive.

Give. Give yourself a chance to breathe, give others a chance you missed. Give presents on holidays, and advice to those who need it, but do not give so much that you have nothing left. Know that some advice you give will not be heeded, and be careful of the ones that are.

And lastly, like circles often do, we have come back to the beginning. As one story ends, another is bound to start. Let close this chapter and start a new one. So stay reckless because twenty years from now, you will look back and be more disappointed by the things you didn't do than the things you did.

lIFe

Dear Life,

Life, is hard. Something new is always coming up, a new assignment, a fight with your best friend, a new guy that will make you eat your heart out because he's with her. It's always something.

Life, is a crazy thing. If the "IF" in the middle doesn't give that away, then, the daily roller coaster should give you a hint. There will never be anything perfect about this crazy, beautiful adventure.

Life, it's about the moments. Live in the moment. Never dwell on what you did yesterday or what you're doing tomorrow. Always be in the moment, because before you know it, the moment will be gone, and you will never of truly lived your life.

Life, it's about the ups and downs. Not every day will be perfect. You will never get everything you want. But, instead of focusing on the nots and the valleys, focus on the dos and mountains. Breathe the morning air, take risks, love forever, and laugh at yourself.

Without appreciation, joy, hope, love, humor, life really isn't worth the journey. Start traveling on the road to the rest of forever. There will be ugly, dead fields, but after, there will be valleys full of flowers and water, you just have to keep strong on the road, the road of life and if.

There is Hope, after all

Reading these letters that people are never going to send makes me realize that so many people are going through the same things I am every day. It's comforting to know that through all of this turmoil and all of this despair, that there can be hope to come of it.

It's like the light at the end of the long dark tunnel.

Open your eyes, you aren't alone. Read some of these letters and realize, too, that even when you think you are all alone in this world and that you've been forgotten, that somebody else is feeling that same way. And even if you don't know them, you can find strength in the fact that you both feel the same things.

And i'm sure that you all will get through whatever is troubling you. It may not be right now, tomorrow, or even next week, but eventually you will heal. And this, whatever "this" is, will not seem so bad at all.

Sincerely,
Someone in the same boat.

What I Wish I Knew In High School

Dear teens ages thirteen to eighteen,

A. Do not compromise your sense-of-self in order to blend in with the crowd; popularity almost always comes with a price, and it's usually not worth it. As trite as it sounds, just be you. Others will like and appreciate you for that. Also, avoid being exclusive in terms of who you choose as friends, because you run the risk of missing out if you don't take the time to get to know those who are viewed as outside of the "acceptable" social parameters.

B. Not everyone is having sex! I know sometimes it might seem like they are, but this is NOT TRUE. A lot of my classmates whom I believed (or assumed) to have been knockin' headboards back in the day actually stayed virgins until sometime later on in college. And a good handful of them, believe it or not, even plan to keep it that way until marriage.

C. One of the smartest decisions I made in high school was to (as lame and project-self-respect-y as it sounds) remain abstinent. It's not like I didn't have boyfriends, and there were definitely opportunities, but I never gave in. Now, at this point I could get up on my high-horse and say it was for some great moral or religious reason, but the simple truth is: I wasn't ready. And as much as I hate making generalizations, I don't think any young teen is quite ready to deal with the emotional and physical consequences of sex. I personally waited until I was twenty-one (and madly in love) to make that commitment. Even as a Junior in college, it can be tough. A lot of new concerns that you never had to think twice about before crop up, and although I'm mature enough to handle it now, I'm not sure I would have been a few years ago. You just shouldn't have to worry about pregnancy, STDs, or comprised reputations (because let's face it, high schools are not exactly gossip/rumor free) at this point in your life. This is your time to be young and free and unburdened with the hardest of adult responsibilities. Don't take it for granted.

D. Try not to get too stressed over GPA's and rankings and SAT's. Everyone has different strengths—don't go crazy comparing yourself to friends and classmates. Do your best, but don't push yourself to the point of exhaustion; the last thing you want is to burn out before college. (If that's the path you plan to take.)

E. Believe it or not, there's life after high school. You're going to meet people who will likely become life-long friends, and you're going to experience new and amazing things. High school is just a stepping-stone to get you to this point; it does not have to set the course of the rest of your life. Enjoy these years, but know that there is so much more waiting just around the corner.

Stop what you're doing and pay attention.

Run. Don't just sit there and stare into space, or watch television, or stuff your face. Don't day dream about her, make up fantasies in your head, or wish she was there. Get off the couch and go get her. Life isn't a movie, you can't just sit there and do nothing and hope it all works out. Love is hard sometimes, it is a trying matter. Call her and tell her how you feel, show up at her house with flowers, or even just pull her aside and talk to her. If she is special to you then let her know. She isn't going to come running through the gate when you're boarding a plane or come busting in right before you say "I do" to the girl you just kinda of liked but decided to marry anyways. Get off your ass and go get her. If you don't, I promise someone else will.

Because It's Worth It.

It's worth it. Every minute of it. Life really is. Think about it. Just take a minute. You may be the most miserable person reading this right now, or happier than ever, but I assure you, it's worth it regardless of how you feel. I don't care if you're Christian, Jewish, Atheist, or whatever you believe. I don't care what your political view is, I don't care if you just made a million bucks or only 50 today at the minimum wage you hate more than anything. Those things don't really matter. Not in the end. Can we really be sure of any end? I don't believe we can, so the best I can do is be as happy as possible for as long as possible. Cause it's worth it! Who knows how long we are going to be here, who knows how lucky we are to be able to experience this? Experience as much as possible!

Take a random trip and get lost, only to find your way back by an adventure. Tell that girl or guy how you feel, because honestly you fail 100 percent of the chances you don't take. And no one likes those chances. I have to say i believe in karma. Those who do good will get good, maybe not now, maybe not in 5 years, but before it's all said and done, those people can say "I am content with dying." And that makes all the difference.

Go to bed every night asking yourself if you'd have any regrets if you had died today. If the answer is yes, make tomorrow better than today. Live it to the fullest! I can't begin to describe to you how important it is. I don't care how much money I have or how good I am at something. I don't worry about what everyone else thinks or what people think of me. We have an incredibly short amount of time on this Earth, and I hope you want to enjoy every minute of it.

You always have a choice. A choice to be happy. But we choose to cry sometimes, or to hide, because we are not strong enough. Well I'll tell you right now you're damn good enough. You're good enough for yourself, and that special someone, and your precious dog that loves you no matter what, and your family no matter what problems they may have.

Don't think everything has been all well for me. Things have gotten bad for me let me tell you. I hate to be negative, but I've been there. I had/have an alcoholic mother. I never knew my real dad. He died a few years ago. I should have two brothers but they died. My uncle committed suicide. But it's ok. It hurts, and I've accepted that. But it certainly is not worth wasting my precious time on this wonderful place. Making the best of it and being as happy as possible is what gives me this outlook and it can to you, I wouldn't be sitting here writing all this otherwise.

You can do it. All of you. If you're already there, great! Spread your happiness! If you're not, you can! I don't know what else to say! There's so much to live for you can even begin to fathom! You just have to start somewhere. Start with telling that person how you feel. Start with going on that roller coaster. Start with sitting out at night looking at the stars. Start with anything that motivates you, and makes you happy! Go from there; go do the next thing that sounds good to you, as soon as possible!

You will find fulfilling your inner motivations and goals and dreams will make you the happiest. And please, I know it's hard, but don't worry about others too much. They don't know better. They are just following everything everyone else has established as "right". Like only being successful if you get A's. Or that promotion. Or hookup with that girl. That's what they want and like to see other people do. If it's really you, great, but if it's not, don't sweat it.

I really could go on all day. Enjoy the little things, and don't ever, don't you ever give up. Because It's Worth It, EF

don't stop

Please don't stop. Don't stop loving. Don't stop caring. Make sure you love yourself enough to survive without anyone. A lover should be something you want, not something you need. Never let them become a need or else you will be destroyed when they leave you. Let them be a part of you, not all of you. I learned this the hard way. Two years and then one day he calls and says he doesn't love me anymore. I made him a need and he made me meaningless. But since then i have become strong. I am whole again. I am not the same person and i will never be as i was. why would i want someone who doesn't want me?

I want to go on a date. I want to be able to kiss someone and feel butterflies. I want to go to bed with someone and then wake up next to them. I want to love again but i know it won't be the same, it never will. The most important lesson that i learned from my heart break is that nothing lasts forever. You can't stop or slow down because life keeps on moving. Love will fade, you will get older, do you want to live with regret? no. Learn to need little and love as much as possible. You are strong. You are beautiful. Go out and Be You because you are an amazing person and people should know. You are a random stranger if you are reading this but know that I love you and wish you all the happiness that life has to offer! GO OUT AND LIVE

For those who are considering suicide.

I love you. I know I might not mean much, but I love you, and I believe in you. Even if you don't believe in yourself, believe in the me that believes in you. I believe that you will make it through this, and I know that you will come through this stronger than where you started. You are worth it, you are beautiful, and you have everything to live for. It may not seem like it now, but if you just wait, if you just don't give up, I know it will happen for you, I know that you will make it happen. I know that every day is a struggle, and I know that you don't think anything will ever change that, but something will. I promise you if you just stick around a little longer, you will find something worth staying for. I don't know your circumstances, I don't know you personally, but I know what you are thinking about doing is not the only answer. You know it too, and I know you know it.

Maybe you've already been to the professionals, and maybe nothing stuck, but if you haven't please do because you are worth it, and your life is worth trying things you maybe didn't believe in. If you have seen professionals, keep trying new ones, because everyone has something different to say, everyone has a different method of working it out, but don't go through this alone. People get through this.

You aren't weak for feeling this way, you aren't a bad person for feeling this way, you are beautiful, and you are special. You didn't know you would be here a few years ago, and you don't know where you'll be in a few years either. Please just allow yourself to believe that there is hope, because there is. Its selfish of me to ask you to do this, I know, but I'm going to be selfish and I'm going to ask you for this favor, and this is all I ever want from you, if that day comes, and you have decided to leave, give it one more day, for me, please. Do something nice for a stranger. I love you so much, don't give up.

You want approval?

Fuck looking for approval.

This is me. This is who I am. And I'll be damned if I ever change myself for anyone ever again.

So to hell with trying to get your approval.

Either you like me or you don't.

You know what, though?

I don't give a fuck.

I fucking approve of me. What about you?

Do you approve of yourself?

-Taking it Day by Day

The carnival of life

Life can be easily compared to most any phenomenon that has a vast meaning. Most people can make that connection of life to anything. Life is a city, life is a meadow, life is a deep forest. I happen to believe that life is a carnival. It only comes around a few times a decade, and is only truly appreciated by some. The colors and noise are what makes up most of our days on Earth. The diversity at a carnival is similar to the diversity of the world. Most people go to a carnival expecting to see or experience a certain feeling, or witness something out of the ordinary. Most people thoroughly enjoy a carnival, as most people thoroughly enjoy life. But occasionally you find people who are just there, wandering and looking for the next best act. Then you have the performers. They are there not because they have a choice, but because they know what they are and enjoy being just that. Lastly there is the ring master. The ring mast is you. Your life, your carnival. You are the ring master. Be the ring master to the best carnival you can, even if it only has 1 act. Make it yours, and enjoy every second of it.

Don't Carry It All

Dear Reader,

I don't understand why you want to grow up so fast. I truly don't get it; don't try to be older than you are. Just enjoy life at whatever stage you're in. Don't forget to do the little things in life that used to make you smile. DON'T FIGHT THE KID INSIDE YOU, HE'S YOUR BEST FRIEND and will help you have some of the greatest memories of your life. Find a friend who helps that kid shine and hang on to them. There will be very few people that you will come across that will do this for you, the majority will force you to grow up and ask you to hide that child deep inside. This, however, isn't an excuse to be immature. Just enjoy life; go run and roll down hills or finger paint or build a life changing blanket auditorium.

Find friends that will help you regardless of the situation. Always remember, friends shouldn't be a constant stressor in your life. They should be there to help you through the stress or to help you forget about it all together. Find one or two great friends and hang on to them. You can have 6000 friends on facebook but when you need help only those real friends will be there for you. I've got my two or three. How about you?

Relationships are tricky. They can be the best thing in your life and they can be your hell. Everyone gets burned; it just all depends on how you carry yourself when it happens to you. You can hate that person until the day you die or you can learn the lessons in the heartache and move on. It's not easy to do but it makes you a better person in the end. Give it a shot.

Things may suck right now, wherever you are in life but just know they will likely get better in the end. This is the first year of really stepping outside of my comfort zone and I can already tell it's changing my perspective for the best. Try it sometime. Try your hardest to take advantage of time as you travel into adulthood. Go for trips, take adventures, make changes while you're young enough to have the time and the ability to enjoy them. "Live every week like it's Shark Week."

Sincerely,
Brutalitops

A note to a new adult.

I know this kid. She's growing into a very wise young woman and all at once she's beginning to notice that the world isn't what she was promised.

Kiddo, this thing is tough. You were told many half truths about the world, how it works and why. People would lead you to believe, without ever saying it implicitly, that this is a great place and a beautiful time to be in it. All around you all you see are these atrocities and horrors and in response to all this you didn't lash out. You did the opposite. You became the kind of person that you thought the world needed more of. I could not be more proud of you. You, one so young, have figured out the trick to changing the world, even if you're unaware of it.

Because it's hard, kiddo. It's hard to just be a human being. Living your life in a polite and good way. Fighting baser instinct to maim and fight and kill. On top of all of this you add the ignorance, the hatred, the bigotry, the senseless violence, the fighting and death over nothing more than money, the paranoia and the general distrust and apathetic way people treat themselves, each other, and knowledge. Because as rough as it gets people exacerbate it. They add to the living hell that is the human condition. I know it's hardly the world you were promised to inherit. I know how far it is from what you thought it was or wanted it to be.

I know how much it hurts to wake up in this hellhole every day and wonder how it'll ever get better. You're on your way though. You're so close you may not even see it. I encourage you, always, to take a step back and look at it from an objective angle. You lost track of your mileage on the journey, but you can always turn around and count the footsteps. Any insurmountable problem has a solution if you can divorce yourself from the consequences of the outcome.

You have the ability and the potential, I can see it in you. You have everything it takes to survive and thrive in a savage world. Sadly you'll need it.

I'm sorry for the deceptions you've been put under, the false pretenses. I'm sorry that I couldn't fix everything before you had to see it in the state it's in. I'm sorry for so much of what has and what will happen.

I trust you to know true right from true wrong. I trust you to make poor decisions and, more so, I trust you to make good decisions more often. I trust you to grow as much as I trust you to protect yourself. I trust your ability to know when to fight and when the time calls for flight. I trust you regarded only the good advice I gave you and none of the bad (more than once anyway.) just as I trust you to be able to make that distinction with all advice.

For all that you've learned and all you will learn the world is a dark and horrible place. The good news is that the half-truths you were led to believe are just that: at least half true. It may not look like it from where you stand, but it's up to you now. You can make your world the place you heard of and dreamed of, or you can despondently accept what you have. It's all up to you to dictate the course of your fate.

But trust me, kiddo. It couldn't be in better or more capable hands. Ignore other people's idea of faith, but never lose faith in yourself. Believe nothing you hear and half of what you read, but everything you say and think. Give help when needed, not when wanted, and accept help when needed and not when wanted. Love as you were shown to love, but only to those that deserve it. Know who really cares for you, and be nice to the people who don't. Be yourself, now and always. You're worth every good thing you get and you're better than all of the bad shit that will be heaped on you. Trust yourself, even if you're wrong sometimes.

You can make your world better. I love you, not because of our relation, but because of the person you are. Never lose yourself. Be good, kiddo. I'm here to help if you need it, and in your case even if you only want it.

Suicide

If you were sitting there, in a cold dark room with a gun in your hand ready to pull the trigger on your own beautiful mind, try to think about where your life would be a year from then if you DIDN'T decide to end your life. Imagine what everything would be like, if you chose to give yourself a second chance. For my best friend Jasmine, who died a year ago at nine o'clock pm on Christmas night I think that a lot would have changed. Now she has no second chance to see where her life would have gone. There is always a chance that things won't get better but for that small slot that it will, you should wait and see. Put the gun down; put the rope back in the garage, close the pill bottle, put down the needle, and see; JUST SEE if your life gets better a year from now. You are amazing, and if you feel like no one would care if you were gone; I WOULD. After losing someone to suicide my heart has created a space that burns every time someone leaves this world by choice. Remember I need you, and so will your future it needs you there to make the amazing life you deserve.

To All the Girls Who Think They Need a Man

You think that your only happiness will come from a relationship. From being wanted, from being admired.

It's true what they say. You can never share in love until you love yourself!

Start a new hobby, pursue a dream, work actively to make your friends smile. Take pleasure in things you can control. The happiest people are those who make others happy. Smile and laugh often.

It's easy to become depressed when you gamble all of your happiness on the actions of a single person. Without knowing it, they can ruin your day simply by not acknowledging you passing by. This is no way to live!

Think about those you admire. Do you ever see them sulking around like you? No of course not! People want to be around happy people because happiness radiates with no more than a cheerful disposition.

Take joy in making others happy. You can control your own happiness if you make the conscious decision to take happiness in the joy of others. It is only then that you will ever find love, when someone wants to be a part of the beautiful change you are making in the world.

Love,
Always

If only you'd realize...

YOU are beautiful.

Yes YOU.

You are worth it.
You are amazing.
Own IT.
Be yourself.
Laugh,
Cry,
Enjoy life because every day might just be your last.
Go off the set path for you and make your own.
Don't have doubts. Doubts turn into regrets. Regrets turn into unhappiness.

Appreciate what you have because one day you might have less. Live in the moment and be free. Love like you have never loved before. Open yourself up to heartbreak. You might find that amazing things come your way.

Because

Dear you,

I want you to know that, when you read this, you are not alone in this world. You aren't the only one that wants everything and anything imaginable. You aren't the sole human being who wants all the hurt to go away. Neither am I.

None of us are alone. No matter how bad you want to deny it, don't. It's comforting, really, to know that. Know that you don't have to accept all the hate in the world, and that change really can make a difference. Believe that tomorrow will be better, will be filled with less hate than yesterday, and understand that some things aren't meant to be understood but are meant to be treasured. Things like love and peace and integrity...things like that are meant to be held on to and never let go.

If you are anything like me, you believe in this too.
How do I know?
Because you are exactly like me, whether you see it or not.

Sincerely,
Someone who cares.

Hope

I'm 14 years old. I haven't done much yet, and I know I have a whole life ahead of me. I want to graduate high school, and go to a wonderful college. I wanted to get married, and have children. I even planned the names already for my future baby boy and girl. Maybe that is my eagerness for the joyous future.

I have a lot of medical problems. Many people shrug it off because I try to conceal the pain. Truly, I want to scream out in agony, I wish to cry and cry until I have no more tears to shed. I try to fight off the pain, tell myself "its alright, you will survive." but what happens when my excuse to convince myself will shatter and become a lie?

I think I will die young.

I do not wish to, and trust me, I will fight and fight for as long as I possibly can. I do not think I will have to prepare for this anytime soon. But I feel as if I will before my dreams have become a reality.

I have met lots of friends in the 14 years I have lived; some of the dearest I have not even met in person yet. They understand and help me through a lot of rough times, when my own parents do not even see it.

Although these lines I write make me cry, for it's hard to see the truth in front of you, I have hope. I will not give up, and those of you, who I understand are going through even harder times, I pray for you. I wish for us all to have faith, and I hope the future will be a wonderful place for us all.

This is to ALL of YOU

To All of You,

How many times have you lied about how you feel? How many times have you regretted walking away, giving up, or moving on? How many times did you want to scream how you felt from roof tops?

How many times did you honestly tell someone what you thought? How many times do you wish someone told you how they honestly felt or what they were thinking?

How many times has it been too late? How many times have you been left wondering?

Far too many times.

Life is scary. There are so many chances to get hurt or to hurt someone else. And as all of you know, being hurt is the absolute worst. Sometimes the pain makes moving on and living life almost impossible. So what if we loved more? Love fully, love fastly, love truly, love always.

What if we told everyone we liked or loved or appreciate or care about just how much we enjoy having them in our life? What if we were more honest about our feelings? What if we have the time now and we waste it?

Why not love and share our love without expecting anything in return? Why not tell your best friend that they truly help you get through the day? Why not tell the barista that they make the best coffee you've ever had? Why not tell that random person on the street that you love their shirt? Why not tell your mom that you love her and appreciate everything she's done for you?

Before it's too late let everyone know just how wonderful they make your life. It'll make them feel better. One less person left to always wonder.

To anyone who's ever yearned for the past

The sad realisation that time really doesn't repeat itself hit me yesterday and that what's done is done and it won't happen again. Sat in a lecture on ethics it really did strike me no wonder everyone is so fed up, down with life, frustrated. Everyone, to an extent, tries to cling on to the past in some way, a happier time perhaps, a moment of content. My happy time was with you, but like in Tess of the D'Ubervilles, 'such happiness can only be short-lived'. Thankfully, I'm not going to be led off to my execution after making that statement, but I am going to be happy.

Memories of the past are great. But don't let them consume you. Pick up yourself, do something for you, and be happy. Whether that's buying yourself a new ferrari, or taking a walk in the woods, stroking your dog, or watching the football. Find contentment and be happy with what you've got.

Yours Sincerely,

A optimistic realist.

P.S, at the time what may seem like the worst thing, may turn out as a good thing. PMA (positive mental attitude.)

beauty in us all

Dear Every Woman,

This letter is for all the women who have ever doubted their beauty. You are not alone. For three years now I have struggled with bulimia.

Some days I look in the mirror and am ok with my reflection. But most days, one glance in the mirror starts a million negative thoughts: "you're obese. you're ugly. no one would look at you." The voice in my head is my worst enemy and in recovery I am trying so hard to retrain my thoughts.

The doctors all say I am of normal weight. I know it's true. Everyone comments that I am stunning. Curves for days in all the right places. So why can't I believe them? Why can't I accept myself and just be grateful that I have a working body? These questions I cannot answer.

I guess my main point is that with an eating disorder it is so easy to feel alone. Like no one understands, like no one cares because it is a shameful disgusting habit. But I understand. And you are NOT alone. Remember this. You are not alone, you are beautiful, and you and I will both beat this.

Sincerely,
Just a Girl

Nice guys? Nice girls? Stop being weak.

Nice Guys.

Grow up. Stop complaining that you'll never meet a girl who won't leave you for a "bad boy" stop complaining that you aren't appreciated. You aren't respected. You are "just a friend."

Nice Girls.

Grow up. You let guys walk all over you. You get cheated on. You get used. You get left behind and thrown over for the girl in the slutty clothes. You aren't respected. You are "just a friend."

Guess what? Nice doesn't mean letting someone else always win. It doesn't mean that what you want is always second place. It doesn't mean you never speak up and take a chance at being told no. It doesn't mean that if you get told no, that that will always happen. Sometimes people just don't feel the way you do. YOU CAN'T CHANGE THAT.

But, you CAN decide what you will do next. Feel worthless or used? Why did you let it go on for so long before you said something? Take it as a lesson. No one gets what they want all the time. That is going to happen to you. It will hurt. It will suck. It will make you feel sad. And it is okay to be down for a little while. But are you really going to be the kind of person who lets one bad result, or several bad results define the way you life the rest of you life?

If it has happened to you more than once, take a look at yourself. Can you respect yourself?

So, Nice Guys. There are no short cuts in life. However, if you skip the "jerk" phase because of how all those girls treated you, and grow up to become a man who knows what he wants and works for it. Who can say no. Who wants to take care of a woman in all circumstances, but not dominate or control her when she goes her own way at times. Then you will find a woman. Not a girl. And trust me. They are better.

And Nice Girls. You date a bunch of jerks and pass over the nice girls because, guess what? you are looking for man. But a real man isn't a jerk to you. he won't be perfect. But he will always try to make you feel perfect. You don't have to put up with domination and control – or the weak willedness of nice guys. You'll find someone who can love you, and respect you, treat you as you do deserve, without giving up his masculinity. But in order for you to deserve them you need to become a woman. It is okay to admit weakness to a man. To lean on them. They NEED to protect you. And you NEED to be able to care for them. Be the one person they know they can lean on and still be a man.

You need a partnership. A we. An us. Not, no girls want a nice guy. Not, no guys want to keep a nice girl. That's fine. Just work instead towards becoming the kind of person worthy of the person you want to be with.

Stop giving up hope. That's weak.

Stop trying to become "bad". That's weak.

Grow up. Be strong. Take your knocks and learn from them.

To What End

Moments can be found in which I deeply question the construct of society, it's all just a self-repeating game. Growing up used to mean getting a job

What they meant to say was growing up was getting in debt, and being disillusioned by the real world.

Why must we always censor things for children, for that matter? There is no reason I couldnt've learned what I've learned now at 14, how much we coddle our children!

The school life is meaningless to a minority, relatively speaking. "Futures" determined by letters, directly proportional to the amount of money made later in life.

Every ancient society of great wealth would erect cities snd buildings of enormous art and stone, nowadays our architecture is practicality disguised as art, all of our workforce is doing generally nothing from 9-5. It's a far cry from the amazing lives we all wish we could live, the ones not filled with so much disenchantment settling for things.

That's the problem with so many people who obtain money, they may often only seek material things with it. I'm always broke and I have relatively nothing to show for it, I spend almost all of my income on experiences; something I think is definitely invaluable.

Success is something so severely out of reach for the majority, and success being proportional to money, money equaling power. The conclusion is obvious, the majority is clearly powerless. All of the people making your food, pressing your clothes, driving your car, for you MR.Ceo, are truly not much more than serfs when it comes to power.

Yet with no need for money, it was those who were gifted with the right place and right time opportunity that could've happened to many others that wind up needing to work the least. The men building his house have to put in an exhausting 12-hour shift. Money, violence, and to a lesser extent, sex, are the tools often used by a society to control its people, for some reason it's just more ethical for the U.S. to dominate its people with money, instead of "third world" countries who use violence.

As long as humans have things to buy, we will always fall for the same trick. Most parents raise their kids on a diet of things, games, toys, phones, things that cost money. Not unlike a dealer trying to get you addicted, no? Then for even more control, the government is allowed to censor our media as well with FCC, ensuring nothing "upsetting" (defined as whatever they define it as) may come on, and the DEA spending 446 dollars a second to keep AWFUL AWFUL drugs that people might recreationally use and enjoy.

But who is so bold to take a step out of the cycle? To live life fully and honestly to his heart's content?

I wish it for everyone. Me included.

Phoenix? That'll be me.

As of today (the 21st of March), there are less than two months until I turn 20.

19 sucked some major ass.

I broke a heart, had my heart broken. Lost a family, gained a family, then lost that one too. Changed my major, shaved my head, pierced my nose. Dyed my hair, found my voice, cried enough tears to fill an ocean. Went to funerals, sang my heart out, lived for the first time. Felt on top of the world, almost took my own life. Was outed as bisexual, got a kitten, tried to breathe. Crashed a car (that most people believe – sometimes, me too– was an attempt to end my life), got another one. Crashed another car (this one an actual accident) which proceeded to catch fire, destroying some of my favorite things to ashes.

I never knew how shattering watching your possessions burning could be. Standing on the side of the road, waiting for the fire engines, staring at the yellow-orange flames lap around something that, until very recently, you were happily driving in. Watching the hat you worked so hard to knit, on needles given to you by someone you loved who died of cancer – burn. Watching the scarf your best friend gave you on the last birthday before she ran away – burn. Watching your schoolbooks and jewelry, perfume and CD's, your car itself, everything – burn.

That's what I feel like I am doing right now. I ran away to get away from a life I didn't want, and now I'm watching this life; the one I thought I wanted, slowly go up in flames.

I've been thinking about dying a lot, lately. I've lost about 30 pounds because I just can't bring myself to eat (I also don't quite have money for food, but even if I did, I wouldn't eat anyways). I haven't listened to music in weeks, because it doesn't bring me joy anymore. I go through the motions while smiling, do the things that a 19 year-old college student would normally do, but then at night I lie in bed clutching my stuffed turtle crying because I don't know what to do.

I feel like I'm in a huge room with tons of doors, and I only have one shot to choose the right one. But the catch is – all the doors are locked, bolted tightly shut. So no matter what choice I make, I'll stay in that room.

I'm afraid that those flames I've been watching are going to reach me in that room and take me down with them.

And then today, it hit me.

I think I've got a plan for what to do, when the fire of 20 comes for me.

I'm going to be a phoenix; break out of that room and rise out of those ashes full of hatred and confusion, of lies and sadness and regret and all of my insecurities.

I really don't intend for this letter (or rather, "inner monologue") to be depressing. I want someone to read this (even just one person, though hopefully I could reach more) and realize one thing. A year, is just a year. A single year out of a lifetime of years. That year might be the worst year ever, like mine seemed to be to me.

But, it's only one year.

For the Dreamers

I have a specific, and large, group of people in mind when writing this letter. It includes every child that ever wanted to be President, or a journalist, or a unicorn rider, or a ballerina, or an actor/actress, or a writer, or an astronaut, or a monkey trainer. It includes every teen that ever dreams, secretly or not so secretly, about what they want to do after college, or even now, right now. It includes every adult that sometimes thinks ("but not SERIOUSLY") about quitting their apartment and moving to Guatemala, or ditching the accounting internship and becoming a fashion designer. It includes everyone in between who has dreams, aspirations, hopes, or whims.

Go for it.

Now, there are winners and there are losers in life-isn't that what we've always been taught? Well, I'm here telling you to flip that saying the bird. There might be "losers", but who the hell says YOU have to be one of them? Just because you have dreams? Now, you know, if you want to be a unicorn trainer you might be outta luck for the moment, but aside from that, seriously, you gotta make it happen, but if you push hard enough, in some form, in some way, it's going to happen. You may need to make some concessions, you may need to compromise, but you can get out. You can make it happen. I promise.

I might just be some starry-eyed poet overburdened by imagination, but hey-it's people like us who make things happen.

You are a dreamer, and whatever it is you're dreaming for... it can happen. You've got to make it happen.

Listen up :)

Dear Writers,

Even though I do not know you, even though I have not met you. I love you. You're all beautiful. For the men and women who think otherwise, stop it. Stop putting yourselves down. You ARE amazing. No matter who you are, where you're from, how how you look. You are all beautiful people, inside and out.

And you think "Yeah, right. How could she know that?"

It's in those words you write, it's in the courage you have when you spill your heart out to the internet, it's the dreams, and the yearning for something more. You are all truly amazing people, every single one of you.

We've all suffered in the past—don't let it ruin your future. It's not easy for me to say this because like some of you, I struggle with the past and how it's affected me today. But don't give in to it, be who you have always meant to have been. Don't get caught up in what happened then. Think of now. Live for now, expand your horizons. Keep fighting for that special something/someone. But remember, nobody holds the key to your happiness-Only you. Only you can make yourself happy. So, get out there and make yourselves happy.

Love & hugs,

From the girl cheering you all on,

Aoi. X

READ TWICE

You know what would be just beautiful? If everyone would just shut the FUCK up and realize that you are most definitely NOT the only person in the world with problems, and that the issues that you do face aren't SHIT compared to what most people have to go through.

Quit crying and whining over facebook, to the people who could give two fucks about anything besides getting a few notifications in regards to their oh so witty status updates, pull your head out of your ass, and fucking grow a pair. Take some responsibility for your actions, and let it be known that the decisions you make today WILL affect the life you are living and the person that you will one day grow to be. Stop playing the victim in every scenario that you can possibly imagine and grow the fuck up.

RESPECT, motherfuckers. Learn it, live it, and surround yourself only with others abiding by this simple rule of life. Bad people can and will eat at your humanity, and then spit it in your face when they have nothing left to take from you. It is important to understand that you are not better than anyone, and that no one is better than you. You only get one chance to bring some meaning to your life, so do the best you can, or get the fuck outta the way. No one but yourself can bring you down, and once you're under, there is not a single soul but your own that can pick you back up.

Remember to remember, and love, love, love. Do not take what you are not willing to give, and stop fucking lying. There is beauty in EVERYTHING; you sometimes have to dig just a little deeper to find it, even if that means tearing deep inside yourself to carve your demons out. Quit being your own worst enemy, and stop being so self-destructive. You are number one in your world, and there is nothing wrong with thinking that. Your sanity and dignity comes before all others, and remember, hopefully they are thinking the same way.

stand up

stand up if you're afraid to die

if you're too lazy to use quotations

if you have searched your whole life to find that one thing to define your life whether it be a movie or a woman or the front bumper of a dodge neon owned by a driver who wasn't quite paying attention

if you go to youtube and click the replay button 500 times a day because itunes is too expensive

if this is keeping you from doing that homework that you really should get to soon

if you have been diagnosed with a disease that makes you feel alienated even though you look down and have hands, feet, fingerprints and even a bellybutton

if you zipper your mouth shut when something bad happens and when you know it's time to open up it's too late and the zipper has rusted shut

if you have been broken up with

if you have broken up

if you have lost someone

if you have found someone

if you can sink a half-court shot with ease but just can't seem to find the handle when it comes to answering the question: what is life?

if you love to sing with head phones in but absolutely cannot stand your voice otherwise

if you love to write and could write all day but losing one poetry slam makes you want to quit

if you have to work 2 or 3 jobs just to put food on the table and put clothes on the backs of your children who you would give every single one of your paychecks just so they can live a semi-luxurious life if you feel like time is spinning

if you're a bookworm who earns an A on all their papers but would like to major in sleeping in

if you have given up on your parents

if your parents have given up on you

if you love your parents so much they are your best friends

if ice cream is your favorite food

if throughout your life time, your childhood was the part you would have loved to skip because of that one single bully who seemed to be the only one standing between you and happiness, and how every day you told yourself at night tomorrow i will stand up to him...

if you were a bully whose childhood would like to be skipped because recess was the only control you had over anything, and going home could never stand up to the nightmares you had as your tears hit the pillow...

if it's hard being a man

if it's hard being a woman

if chocolate gives you acne

if you respond "i live" to the question "what do you do for a living?"

this is a letter i will never send to any single person because when it comes down to it, we all will be standing, whether we are three years old chasing the ball into the road or eighty-seven surrounded by love ones. life shouldn't be a comparison of who's right or who's wrong but about what you have done to get there. so stand up now and go forward

You can do this

You, you can do this, just get up and try. It might be the hardest thing in the world, but that does not matter, do it. you'll feel better after. You'll improve your mind, body and soul. Just go! Yes it will hurt, yes you will be sore, yes you will be the worst one and everyone will be better, more flexible, thinner, stronger, better in every way, but just go. You'll feel better, you'll feel like a million bucks after, so just go! Go, go, go and go until it hurts go, go, go until you think you can't, go until you fall and then get up and go tomorrow too, the next day, and the next. Every day, Every day and every day will get better than the next, until one day you heal your heart.

You deserve better

Dear teenage girls,

Life is so much more than high school. I can't stress that enough. It gets so much better. In your life, you'll find love like you've never imagined, if you'll only trust and believe in yourself.

Let go of those abusive, tumultuous, violently passionate flings. When they're good, they're amazing. I know this, because I've been there. But they're not meant to last. They are learning experiences. The heartbreak that he brings you will make you stronger and will prepare you to be the independent, beautiful woman that will one day be loved by the man that you probably don't believe exists.

I know because I've been there. Now in my twenties with a promising career, I look back on my teenage years. On the years spent in beautiful, feverish love affairs. Those years were far from wasted time. Never would I say "I wish I had never met (insert name of ex-boyfriend here)."

Each unhealthy experience has made me the woman I am today. The woman who is now able to fully appreciate the man with whom I've fallen in love. He is the knight in shining armor that I dreamt of as a girl. There ARE men out there who are more than just lust-filled, hormone driven machines. I know because I've found one.

There ARE men who will make love to you, instead of just "fucking". There ARE men who will kiss you on the forehead just because they love you. There ARE men who will write you love letters— who will build you bookshelves— who will put their pride aside for the sake of your love— who will put everything on the line for you— who will make themselves vulnerable to your attacks. Do not give into the urge to attack him. He is not the boy of your teenage years.

When you meet him, he will be a man. And you will be a woman, not because you have grown older, but because you have grown wiser.

Signed,
Someone who has been there

Love

Every day is different. Nothing is known beyond the moment we are living in, right now. All you can do is live to your fullest and treat every day as though it's your last. Take risks. Do all the things that "when I'm older I'm gonna do this" well your older, so do it. God is always gonna be with you. EVERYTHING will turn out how it's meant to. It's all in His plan. You're gonna find "the one" one day. Because there is a "one" for everyone. Everyone has "the one". Some are just harder to find than others.

Never stop believing in yourself.

Never fear.

Never give up.

Get up every morning, breathe, and smile.

It's gonna be okay.

You're not alone.

~Me

We are connected

I am sitting here in my little town called Reilingen/Germany and I'm writing this note to you and you know it is for you because you are reading it right now! Remember, there are no accidents – everything happens for a reason. You and I are no different I'm you and you are me, eternal consciousness individuated in the form of me and the form of you. We are made of the same stuff and we are both – all of creation is – the one eternal ISNESS that plays itself out as you and me and everything there is. You are Love not fear, and if you have forgotten who you are, I am reminding you right now how wonderful you are. You, my friend, make a difference in this Universe. Without you, the weaving of creation would not be the same anymore. I'm glad that you exist, that you chose to be here in this time-space continuum. Namaste, my friend, the spirit in me is greeting the spirit in You. I hope you find your own precious way of being and expressing yourself in this world. It is good that you are here. Enjoy the ride and never forget you and God are forever ONE! In fact WE ARE ALL ONE!;)

Our Own Kind of Beautiful

Dear little girl who looks at older girls and wants to grow up to be just like them,

You won't. You will not be just like your beautiful cousin or babysitter or aunt. I know it's tough. All you want is the same beauty that they ooze everywhere they go, but you'll grow up and when you do, you'll realize that you're nothing like them.

Maybe, at first, you'll be disappointed. Hell, who am I kidding? You might be disappointed your whole life. Many girls are. Even that beautiful babysitter or cousin, who you imagine must be the most beautiful girl you've ever seen, may be disappointed about her looks. Don't be. Never look in the mirror and imagine how much prettier you would be if only your hair were curly, or if only your nose were a little smaller.

I'm not saying that you're perfect. I'm not saying anyone is. But you are beautiful and you will grow up to be beautiful and someday you will fall in love and someone will think that you are the most beautiful girl in the world.

Most importantly, please believe you are beautiful. Someday, you will grow up and a little girl will see you and think to herself that she wants to be as beautiful as you are. You have to believe that you're beautiful, so that you can tell her this and it will keep her going long after she's lost faith in fairy tales.

You are beautiful and you will grow up to be beautiful and I know that you always will be beautiful. Don't forget it.

Sense of Dread

It's dark and trying and feels like the end; going on seems pointless. Every ragged breath you take burns and catches, turning living into a chore. It will never be any different, never any better than it is now, like some thunderous cloud is hovering above your head waiting to let loose. You start to accept the fact that you will always have this ever-present sense of dread and sorrow and then it happens. It gets better. No specific reason, no big showdown, life just improves and you're stuck wondering how you let something so small dictate so much of your life. You smile and it feels so easy, natural. When you're in the pits of belittling self-worth life turns into something you have to endure but it gets better, it always gets better, you just have to hold on long enough to realize that.

this is not your sign

Dear everybody who's waiting,

These days, everybody's waiting. Waiting for 5 o'clock to roll around, waiting for a better job, waiting to belong, waiting to find themselves, waiting to lose themselves, waiting for the weekend, waiting to fall in love, waiting to fall in love, waiting to fall in love, waiting for the spring, waiting for school to end, waiting for school to begin, waiting for hair to grow, waiting to grow up, waiting for the next paycheck, waiting for the perfect person, waiting to leave home, waiting to come home.

But listen; yesterday is merely an idea invented by nostalgic humans and tomorrow will never exist. And the ability to dwell in an imaginary future is crippling our society. Our minds are exhausted from existing in so many places at once, and the masses are scared into stagnancy by "what ifs" and "maybe tomorrows". Because if you can't make it happen today, then you sure as hell can't make it happen tomorrow. And the security we thought we found in 'plans' is slowly crushing us.

Listen. You need to hear this; tomorrow will never come. It always has, is, and will be today. Our generation's biography could be filled with nothing but "one day I'll's..." Listen. This is your day. If you were waiting for a sign, this isn't it. Because signs are like fairies and soul-mates. There are no eagles in the sky, or voices from above, or magic old beggars.

It's about time we realized that each and every one of us has to be our own sign. The timing is never going to be right, the money is never going to be there, your courage will never feel like enough. But it is. Because someone is always going to be whispering no, or maybe even shouting. Someone will always tell you it's foolish. Naive. And they'll be right. But what good ever came of cynicism and disillusionment?

Go make mistakes, your mistakes are beautiful. They are as lovely as you. Live. Don't just exist. Don't ever let yourself be taken captive by the mundane. Don't ever let routine get its fingers around your neck, because it won't let go. For once, immerse yourself in the present. Listen; tell him you love him, get on that plane (or train), read that book, shave your head, stop wearing shoes, eat that weird tentacle sushi, go dumpster diving, talk to that stranger, say what you think every once in a while, go to australia, be naked, go to college, drop out of college, let yourself scream, let yourself be silent, take a risk, JUMP.

Listen; waiting isn't even a real word. It's an impostor. It mocks the very essence of a verb. It is the absence of action. Forget you ever knew what it meant. Live a life of motion, not lack thereof.

Could it be any better?

When you stop and breathe. Take in what you see.

Take in what's real.

Thoughts wander, ideas torment,

Laughter heals, and time prevails.

I love how I can forget you...

I forget you and you come back...

I moved on, and you decide you did not.

Love is not real; love is not what we had.

Your thoughts wander into your ideas that torment me

My laughter made me heal, while time prevailed in my head.

Isn't true? It is never darker when it is time for dawn...

Could it be any better?

I understand.

To every girl out there who has ever had her heart broken—

You aren't alone. And honestly I know how much it hurts. I miss him too, and every day that goes by you wonder if there was something you could've done differently. Something that might've changed his mind, or stopped him from cheating, or kept his interest.

I know how special he made you feel. I know how he held you. I know how he loved you.

All I can really say is that I don't know when we'll move on, or when we will find a better guy. All I can say is, I hope that time comes soon. Because there isn't one girl in the world who doesn't deserve it.

Keep faith. And, when it feels like no one cares, remember I still do. I know how you feel and like I said before, you aren't alone.

Life is

Life is,

Life is unique. It is beautiful in its simplicity and complexity. Life pulls at the fabric of my inner-self pushing me to become better than the best I'll ever be.

I will be better because I have to be; I choose to be.

You are so beautiful in many ways and I will never get to be with you. But this is exactly how it is supposed to be.

all plays out just as it should, but my tears say otherwise.

I am searching for and driving towards a reason I am not sure exists.

I will be full of joy.

I choose to brighten the world because I can and I feel that that is what you would like me to do, and I suppose it makes me feel good deep down as well.

Life is pretty awesome when you think about it though.

How Many Steps?

My name is Victoria and I spend every single day counting the number of steps that I take. If I ride a bike I count the number of times my legs complete a rotation on the pedals. If I am riding a scooter I count the number of times I push with my left leg but never my right. On a skateboard I count the amount of times I pump and then divide it by the seconds I spend coasting. No one knows this and I doubt anyone will ever find out.

Have you ever wondered why it might take you 237 steps to get to a 7-eleven one day and the next only 214? That's why I count my steps. I want to know what those little things are in your day that no one can explain or notice that cause one to shorten their walk by an entire 23 steps. 23 whole freaking steps! I mean that probably seems like nothing to you. That's hardly a change in your routine. But that's why I count my steps. I notice all the little things people don't. Those little things you ignore are invisible to the naked eye.

See that squirrel that just ran across the sidewalk and caused you to jump? Yeah, that's another step. That's another deviation from your normal routine and that change might make the biggest difference or alter nothing at all. So next time you wave hi to a friend, hold a door for someone, spit in the grass, smell the roses, poop in a public restroom, drink a latte, remember all the little things you can't see. Those are the spirits that you learn to feel, learn to read and learn to follow their intuition. Unknowingly they guide you throughout your day and create the path that you end up living. So take a minute and listen, count your steps because what you don't notice is what matters the most.

Believe

This is for the girls who have cried themselves to sleep over a boy who never cared. For the girls who try and try again and yet always seem to fall short. This is for you innocent, naive girls who believe every word he has and ever will say. This is for the girls who would rather stay in on a Friday night, reading books about any life other than their own. This is for the girls who try to hide behind make up and short skirts. For the girls who cannot see their own beauty every time they look in the mirror. For the incredibly intelligent girls who are afraid to let their light shine through. For the girls who believe that boys only date the dumb, "hott" girls. This is for the girls who stay up late reading letters on the internet trying to find something to believe in. This is for the girls who look through his pictures even after he told you, you two were better as friends. For the girls who don't know how to be something he'll miss. For those of you who have stopped believing in love. Who have stopped believing in anything greater than themselves, I have a message for you.

It gets better. Some day you will reach outside of your small town and realize that all the little things don't matter anymore. You'll grow up and learn that falling short only makes you stronger. And being intelligent and hardworking is not something to be ashamed of; it's something to be proud of. Your motivation and will power will be something that will get you far in life. Some day you will meet the man of your dreams and he'll turn your life completely upside down. He will respect you and make you want to be an even better person than you've already become. Soon you'll realize that those short skirts and drunken hookups with have done nothing for those other girls. It will only make their futures harder. Stay strong, stay pure, and keep believing in yourself. Love is out there. Your life will begin to fall into place and you'll look back at your awkward teenage years and laugh. You'll laugh because you know that all of those hardships have only grown to make you stronger.

You are beautiful. You have a strength inside of you that no one else can match. You will change the world.

You.

Dear you,

We all have our days where we feel depressed, forgotten, or alone. We all have our days where we feel lost, or confused. Angry or betrayed. But let me assure you something-you are far from alone. There are many people out there just like you that feel the same way you do, whether it's good, or bad.

If you're on the point of breaking down and wanting to end your misery, please, don't. You are beautiful, inside and out, and though you may not hear it every day, there is someone who thinks it every day. This is something interesting to think about-there is someone out there looking for you. Someone is looking for you to marry, start a life with, and grow old together. Don't throw all that away because of a rude comment someone said to you this morning at school, or a group of immature girls is wasting their time bullying you. They will not break you. You are a strong person. I have faith in you that you will ignore all your enemies' remarks and remind yourself that you are a unique individual with potential to do anything you want to do in life. Don't give up everything you've worked for because of one comment, or even several comments. People's opinions about you shouldn't mean anything, because all it takes is one positive comment to make you happier, whether you want to admit it or not. There is someone out there who would worship the ground you walk on just to be with you. There is someone out there who loves you and thinks you are the most beautiful person they have ever seen. YOU ARE AN AMAZING PERSON AND NOONE SHOULD TRY AND BRING YOU DOWN. People who hate on others are immature, insecure little children who are bored with their own lives, or unhappy with their own lives, and they are going to do everything in their will to bring you down. Well-put up a fight and block out their harsh comments. They aren't true. If you read this, first of all I want to say congratulations because you actually made it through the entire paragraph of my comments, and second, remind yourself that no one out there is better than you, and someone out there would die to be everything you are. No matter how sad you may be, or whatever your case is, you are loved and appreciated by someone in some way.

Have an amazing day, and don't let anyone bring you down.

For the people who never give up

Sometimes in life it seems that we are too focused on watching the hands on the clock tick by and seeing that time go by so fast yet doing nothing of any importance. You are brilliant and intelligent and funny and I honestly believe there isn't a thing in this world that you cannot do with the right amount of will. But... We are afraid...of stepping too far outside the 21st century norm. So much so that we don't even bother looking down at the lines that blur between our feet... the lines that divide us into our labels that we wear like heavy burdens on our backs.. Freaks. Handicaps. Fatties. Skeletons. Idiots. Emos. Chavs. We are ALL human... And we are all truly amazing and individual and oh, so so beautiful. Do NOT let anyone tell you otherwise. please, for me?

There are times in life where sometimes we are ignored and abused and just left out and often we forget that there is a whole lot of world left out there for us to find. We could all just spread out and find the place we feel we belong and never look back to the small towns we came from. So, you think you are stuck now... but just hold on, I mean... you can go anywhere you want after the age of 19. It seems like an awfully long time but... the wait is worth it, and the situations you hate now will give you wisdom many people older than you often do not acquire because they did the wrong thing and ran from their lives and often ran so fast that they couldn't stop to see the beauty of the small things in life.

NEVER do that. never wake up and go about a day without first looking out your windows, taking in the day and greeting it with one of your dazzling smiles. Then, go to the mirror and smile at yourself and let your brain tell your heart there is someone out there for you. There is always someone for everyone. Don't ever lose hope over small things like that. I promise, when you stop worrying, things start changing for the better, you are a beautiful person. And there is enough light inside each of us to light the minds of strangers and everyone else in our lives. You truly are amazing. I'm 15 and I'm telling you something you need to know for the rest of your life. Don't let my words go to waste x

You Need to Know This

It'll hurt. I'm bracing you now, because I know some foolish part of you is going to hang on till the very end, go down with your sinking ship, but I want to warn you; it'll feel like a punch in the stomach, like a kneed to the face. There will be bruises and blood and fire left behind; these kinds of explosions aren't subtle. Shrapnel will fly and lodge itself in your chest. You'll have scars.

You're going to wonder if it was worth it.

The bitter part of you will say no, but in reality it was. Because sometimes you need to love blindly and hopelessly. Sometimes you need to hurt just to know you're still feeling, just to know that you are still alive.

(He kept you alive, didn't he?)

Because sometimes we need to jump without the hope of flying to be reminded of gravity.

After the heartbreak, life will go on. Even for you.

my advice

Dear whoever YOU are,

People ask me for advice. All the time I'm posed with "What should I do?" or "Why does this happen to me?" or, worst of all, "What should I think?"

I don't know why they ask me. They say it's because I'm wise and they trust me. I don't know why they'd say that, it's almost the most ridiculous statement I've ever heard. My life is a mess, I don't know what I'm doing, and I'm not smart enough to care.

Nonetheless, here is my advice. Do the stupidest thing you can think of. The most important things in life are the ones that society deems a waste of time. Go ahead and look like a fool! It's the most fun you'll ever have. Have an adventure, and have no regrets. I don't pretend to know what I'm doing, but I don't care. It really doesn't matter what you do half so much as that you did it.

But, whatever you do, do it for the sake of love. I don't mean mushy gushy stuff, or middle school romances. I mean, find the part of this world that you love with more of you than you even knew there was, and live for that. Be stupid for it. It'll be worth it, I promise.

A note for someone who wants to listen

I guess I never realized how unexpected life truly is. Reading all these letters has made me realize that we are all human beings struggling to get by in a world full of chaos, love, uncertainty, tears, and smiles. I am 19 years old; I am young, inexperienced, and learning. My entire life I have been with different guys, not in a promiscuous way. The reason I have talked to so many different guys is because I don't believe at times that I am worthy enough to deserve anyone at all. I talk to guys, get close to them, and let them go. I have never had a long term relationship, never gotten close enough to a guy to trust them with my darkest secrets, and I have never let a guy love me. It's strange though, my parents are amazing role models. They're two individuals who are deeply, in everlasting love with one another. I went to a psychic a few months back; right away she read that I don't let men into my life. Why? I have no idea. I am working on it, and I pray one day someone will enter my life, will change my life, and will teach me how to LIVE my life. A special note for any of my readers, appreciate those who offer you love. Love is what keeps our universe connected. It's what produces happiness, smiles, tears, and sorrow..... it's what produces EMOTION.Without experiences all these different obstacles and forms of emotion, we would never know LOVE. Let yourself be emotional, let yourself into people's lives, take risks, and live a little. If you have had that special someone you always wanted to call, kiss, or express your inner buried feeling for.... GO FOR IT. What do you have to lose? You never know until you try. We have one shot in this world, and nothing is guaranteed.

This is for you, yes you.

To those struggling to let go, you need to read these words.

It pains us all, but sometimes we meet people we can liken to our own individual form of a disease. They infest all our thoughts, put pressure on our hearts, and exhaust us. Allegedly, these people are the ones we adore, the ones we persist to refuse to let go only because we are too scared to face things alone. The truth is that these very people are the ones that will drag you down, they will let you wallow in your own self-pity as they revel in how you miss them, they will use you because they know you will always be there, and they will deprive you of happiness for they refuse to let you be happy with anyone else. We all let these people walk into lives, we are so blinded by love that we are oblivious to the poison they inject into us, that slowly destroys what we have worked so hard to become. You will suffer, you will let them manipulate you, you will let them take away every fibre of who you are in order for them to lay down a path of happiness for themselves.

Never forget who you are, never let them take what makes you a better person. Never let them make you believe you can't be loved. You deserve better, and you will find better.

Life

Hey there, honestly, i don't know you, i'll never meet you, and i might even pass you one day on the street and i won't even know it's you. but i don't care about that. today is a good day. it's a beautiful day. you make it possible. everything we do, every day is all in thanks to you. i love you for it. i don't mean that bullshit that people say when they mean just to say it. i mean i love you for you. for being a human being, for existing, for crying, laughing, jogging and dancing. i love you. without you, we wouldn't be here. everything everyone does is somehow thanks to what you do. if people say you're worthless, shitty, or something else. then just smile. perhaps even laugh a little on the inside and chuckle. laughter is one of the many beauties of life.

be who you want to be. don't do things because society dictates it and because it's a social norm. be who you want to be and who you are. gay, straight, hipster, gangster, mobster or smoothie mixer. do what you want to deep down. don't care what other think of you, because those that do don't matter and those who don't care matter.

live your life to the fullest. we are all scared of death. perhaps we're all scared because we haven't lived our lives to what we would have. don't do anything in your life that will make you think in the future "if only". life is an adventure. as we grow older, we somehow lose that. be spontaneous, adventures, perhaps even a bit of a rebel at times. live life so that one day, when you in that bed in the hospital with all of those tubes sticking out of your arms, nose and what not, or sitting by the shore of a lake, you can look back, smile and hopefully, have no regrets. we don't live for the goal we seek at the end. if you do, then the little surprise is death followed by a new life. it's all about the road you take, whether you wander from it and maybe climb a tree while going there.

religion. what is it? honestly, it's all the same to me. whether you call him Allah, Jehovah, Brahman or god, he is all the same. we often fail to realize that all religions follow the same outline; they just have different names for their gods and saviors.

all you need is love. it's honestly one of the most, or even the most beautiful thing i can think of in life. once you achieve love, you will realize what you have been waiting for your whole life. you feel as though you can lift the mountains and swim the oceans. love will make the weakest man invincible, and the strongest man crippled. love hurts, breaks and makes. sure, you will experience pain with love, a lot of us have been there and done that. but that doesn't mean that we should stop fighting for it. the most beautiful things in life are often the hardest to get. whether it's love for your wife/husband or your family, it's all worth it.

none of us can understand life. hell, i hardly even understand mine. don't be a blind ant mindlessly wandering around just doing what everyone else is. do what drives you and compels you. we can't understand life and we never will. if you can't accept that, then you're a fool. it's all about living it and enjoying it.

for now, that's all i can really say. just be you, because without you, none of us will ever be the same. live, laugh, love

The Struggle

They say there is only ever one religion. They say money solves everything. They say they are right, and only them. Life isn't about them. It's about you. You only live once. Or maybe not. No one knows, and that's the point. The point is if we give into it all, let ourselves be swept up into the "them", you die. Every day, you die a little more, simply because you lose yourself. Don't accept others ideas, simply because they say it's true. Don't be afraid to stand out. Don't be afraid to say your opinions. Don't let age, sex, religion, race, or size hold you down. YOU are the only person that matters. Because I can guarantee one thing. When it all comes down to it, you'll be regretting not what you did, but what you didn't do. This monologue was written by a thirteen year old girl. In summation? Don't let other people tell you what to do.

Never good enough

Dear Anonymous Reader,

It may be 2:03 am. It may be a Saturday night when most people are out having fun. It may be just another night alone for you. It may be as it is for me; and maybe that thought alone is enough to pull you through the loneliness. You are not alone in your lonesome. We can be alone together. That may not take the edge off the longing. That may not fix a thing, but the thought that you may be alone too is enough to pull me through.

We're all looking for a reason to pull through. So whatever plagues your thoughts tonight, know you are not alone and you are loved by some blue eyed no one living in a town called normal. It's in Illinois if you don't believe me.

Sincerely,
Anonymous Writer

Dear person reading this...

Whether you're a girl, or a guy. I want you to know that you're loved. Someone out there loves you more than words can describe!

Whether you just broke up with your boyfriend/girlfriend, you can make it through this. It might seem like the end of the world, but before you had them, you survived, didn't you? You made it through the tough times by yourself. You're strong enough.

I have faith in you.

Whether you're 1 or 100, You're capable of ANYTHING you put your mind too. You just need determination.

Whether you feel like you're nothing. You're special to SOMEONE out there. Someone who feels like they can't live without you.

Whether you're me, or some stranger reading this. You have a GREAT deal of determination. You just have to find it within yourself.

And Trust me. You can make it through anything!?

TO ALL THE GIRLS LOOKING FOR SAPPY LOVE LETTERS

This isn't it. I want each and every one of you to know you are absolutely stunning. If you think you need a counterpart to feel this way, think again. You are so much stronger than you realize and you don't need to be connected to someone to feel safe. I'm not bashing love, trust me I believe in all of the crazy beautiful miracles love can bring people. However, making the decision to be single has made me love myself more than I ever have in my life. I've never been able to 'find myself' and all that jazz, really know who I am, what I want, or where I'm going, because my time, energy, and most importantly- my thoughts were all spent on significant others. So I'm here to tell you to make time for yourself. Don't let your youth or your life be spent on a quest for a partner. When you embrace yourself completely I promise you 100% they will find you. It's only then that someone will be able to fully fall for you, because you will be the truest you you can be.

From me to you.
With love.

Beautiful...truly

To the woman who is reading this:

If you are young, teenaged, middle-aged, elderly, wrinkled, freckled, light-skinned, dark-skinned, tall, short, curvy, petite...whatever....just know that the unique combination of those types of words is exactly what you are....UNIQUE.

Dear, you are BEAUTIFUL! I am amazed by you even though I have never met you. You have such a great smile, a light in your eyes, and a personality that is like an original work of art- it might try to be replicated, but it can never be the same. Media is WRONG; you are a well-made, strong, intelligent, lovely woman. Don't forget that!

Remember that looks will fade and that people are not perfect; there is no such thing as "perfect beauty", so don't let anyone or anything tell you that you must be this, that, or the other to be considered beautiful and desirable. YOU ARE! Stop being so critical! You are fine the way that God made you, and someday, someone else will believe you are the mostly exquisitely crafted person put on this planet.

People that say mean or negative things are insecure of themselves and are threatened by your beauty....because girl you've got it! You are a MASTERPIECE! Tell yourself that each day. When you get ready to leave for school/work/wherever, look at yourself in the mirror and compliment yourself, buy pretty panties (they make a difference), feel sexy because you are sexy, do something for YOU every now and then, and when someone insults you, try your hardest to smile or even say a compliment back: a lovely and kind soul is a beauty that never fades or goes out of style.

So remember....you ARE beautiful...truly.

Sincerely,
Another Woman

live life love

Hello, there.

I've never met you and I probably never will. Right now we could be on other sides of the planet, or right down the street. When this is published, I may have forgotten about it. I may be walking through my day as usual, but sometime in the future, someone will read this. And hopefully, someone will smile.

That someone is you. Because right now, from where I sit typing this, you are the person I'm thinking about. The person I'll never know, reading a letter written miles and miles away. Some might say I'm writing this to no-one in particular, but really, I'm writing this for you.

There's a reason why you're reading letters never sent properly, and somehow it led you to this one. I hope that the reason is something lovely. I hope that you're reading these letters because you want to be inspired. I hope that you're reading these letters because you want to smile, because damn it, that's my wish right now. That you'll find what you're looking for, that it's not an impossible goal, that there will be a smile on your face by the time you're finished reading.

You've made it this far, and for that I am amazed and thankful. And if you're reading these letters because you feel lost, the way I am whenever I read pages and pages biting back tears, I'll try for some advice:

Love is love is love. Love yourself, love others. Love is not wrong.

Travel. Leave everything but a bag and go somewhere, if only for a day. Breathe in new air.

Live life. Your life is a gift, a miracle of science or luck or God or whichever you believe. Don't hold back, don't live for others. Live for yourself. Because you, love, you are the most beautiful person in the world, and I am writing directly to you as I say this, as I say that maybe your life is rough right now, but it has so much potential. You have so much potential. Live your life the way you want it lived, because on your dying day, you won't be worried about what your parents or your girlfriend or your boyfriend or your friends thought of your life, you'll be looking over it and wondering, 'What have I left?' Is it worth the life I lived?

The answer should be yes, love, because if you're not living your life now, today is the day to start.

So many people only breathe and walk and sleep and eat. So few people live. And it'd break my heart to see you one of the former.

Have you smiled yet, love?

Maybe we'll meet one day. Maybe I'll have you smile then.

Until next time,
AK

For the Undergraduate

I hope you never stop yearning for knowledge.

I hope you strive for individuality although conformity is an easier path.

I hope you will always continue to question; question all that you hear and all that you believe.

I hope you speaking for your mind will not be as difficult as discovering your own voice.

I hope memories will be made.

I hope you will persevere through the troubling days and never forget to congratulate yourself at the end.

I hope living life to its fullest is not a wish but a guarantee.

I hope through everything you discover, everything you experience, and in all the ways that you will transform, you will always know who is beside you.

I hope these days will bring you light towards your future. Everyday wake up and remember...your future is bright. It is right in front of you. Believe in yourself.

To Whom It May Concern:

You're beautiful.

You're passionate about life.

You have dreams that you don't know how to make come true.

You doubt yourself at times.

You're scared.

You don't love enough.

Here is your medicine, your remedy, your way out of this hole you're in.

Repeat after me, "I am beautiful." – say this every morning.

Sing at the top of your lungs.

Make your bed, and then jump on it!

Eat what YOU want.

Tell at least one person "I love you" every day.

Give a stranger a compliment. It does wonders when that person is you.

Pay for the person behind you in the drive through. It's a good selfless deed.

Learn to love yourself and your life, no matter what comes your way.

I believe in you, I hope you do too.

<3

It's not what you got but what you make of what you've got

Hey....Life is a struggle but I've learnt that it's the way you actually think of it that matters. You can see every trouble as something that will put you down and drag you to hell or you could see every trouble as an experience that will teach you not to make that wrong decision that led to what happened to you. Yes, sometimes it's not your fault that something happened but life is short and you need to forget about those things that you just can't control.

School has many challenges and friends are the biggest challenge, you can never be sure if what they show the world is what they actually are. Still it doesn't mean you should not make new friends because although the world is full of bad people there are good people out there like you and me.

Despite the fact that love and friendship break hearts you need to love and care, what is life without it? We should love expecting nothing in return, do good even if it goes unappreciated and don't judge people.

Be nice, it never hurts to be nice. Be the first to say sorry, even if you have to say it every time; but stand up for yourself and don't be a doormat. No-one deserves to be treated like they don't belong. Stand up for that kid who is bullied every day, one day you'll be glad you did it.

Tell yourself you're amazing, others shout your faults but only whisper your greatness, so know that everyone in the world has flaws, shout to yourself your greatness and forget about the faults unless you can do something about them.

Don't regret decisions even if they gave you the wrong results. Be confident. I believe that "it's not what you got but what you make of what you got" that really shows personality.

Lots of Love,
The Optimist

To You.

You're beautiful. I don't know who makes us, if it's god or genetics. But you're such a beautiful gift to the rest of the world. And I'm sure many people realize you're beauty every day. Most boys are just too shy to say it and girls are just too envious to admit it.

Don't forget, that life is a beautiful, beautiful thing. And that every day is a gift. Don't sit cooped up in your room all day, depressed about politics and who's gonna predict the end of the world. It doesn't matter! There is a whole world out there that you're missing! So breathe in the air, let the sun dance on your face, and listen to the birds sing. Do it to remind yourself that you are alive and...

A gift. Because you are. You bring something to the table that no one else can. Your humor. Amazing charisma. Weird dance moves. Shy disposition. God-like grace. Sweet smile. Surf Skills. Ability with animals. Awesome piercing technique...something! You are a gift to the world and down to the dimples you get when you smile, you have something that everyone knows you by. So embrace it. It's something that defines you.

And don't ever forget, you are important. You have worth. And even if you don't realize it or don't believe it, there are people out there that love you. And they need you. And the thought of life without you would change their life. Because you are a beautiful, talented person and bring something to the world that wasn't here before you.

Sincerely,
Emily

people that travel by plane

dear travelers,

i fly every month.

several times a month.

i write letters to you dear travelers every time I fly.

they change every time, but they always mean that someone is there for you. no matter what.

you are never alone. you are with me and everyone else in this world.

in their pain, happiness, loneliness, excitement, and wanderlust.

i hope you keep these letters, or read them and keep them there to share, or start to write your own.

but if you ever see a paper lined and has swirlies on it, written in black sharpie, folded in half, signed "-K" that's me.

i'll never stop. i'll never lose touch. and i hope that i have helped someone. somehow. someway.

-K

Thoughts from One Soul

Hey everyone. I'm a young adult, on the brink of entering the real world. I think a lot, most would say too much, until my insight becomes a bit of a burden. I used to think of my mind as a curse, and sometimes I still do. But now I am starting to appreciate the way I think for what it is-my philosophical nature, my appreciation for beauty and art, my endless curiosity. All this can be used for good. Thinking doesn't have to destroy you. It can cause things to spring into life in your mind. I am trying to only use my thinking for positive outcomes now. It is a new habit that is slowly developing.

But first, I would like to confess a few things about my life, and share them with all of you:

I have felt very alone and very different. I have always felt one step removed from everyone I have met. It is sometimes a terrifying and isolating feeling. But I am starting to think we all are like this, and are aware of it in varying degrees. I am very aware of my own solidarity, one life and one soul among so many.

When I was little I was very sick and no one knew what was wrong with me. My earliest memories are of hospitals and ambulances. It turns out I was exposed to harmful chemicals in my school. I have completely recovered, but it has left me with intense hypochondria and increased anxiety about being a hopeless case that can't be fixed.

When I was 12 I started having my first panic attacks and suicidal thoughts. I didn't tell a soul. It was the loneliest and darkest period of my life. When I was 16 I was sexually assaulted. I felt like it was my fault. I felt violated and strange. I didn't tell a soul. I'm still weird in relationships.

When I was 18 I left for college. The stress of the transition brought up everything I had never dealt with and I had a mental breakdown and took a leave of absence from school. I returned the next semester after seeking help in the form of therapy. And I am doing well, several months later.

If you have ever felt like absolutely no one in this whole world could understand what it is like to be you, I HAVE BEEN THERE. If you have ever felt like it was hopeless, like you couldn't stand the idea of the rest of your life, I HAVE BEEN THERE. If you have ever harmed yourself in any way, I HAVE BEEN THERE. I HAVE ALSO COME BACK. And trust me when I say I truly never thought I would.

Yes, life is a constant struggle. Things don't just become rosy and happy all the time. But you learn not to be afraid of what you can't control. You learn to accept that we are all alone, in a sense, but we still have each other. You learn how to make the way you are work for you, because it's going to have to work. You have no other choice. You realize that things take time, sometimes a lot of time. Life is a process.

I wish you all the best. You are not alone. I will end this note with a quote from the fabulous film V for Vendetta that I have always loved:

"But what I hope most of all is that you understand what I mean when I tell you that even though I do not know you, and even though I may never meet you, laugh with you, cry with you, or kiss you,? I love you. With all my heart, I love you. -Valerie"

Where I Lived and What I Lived For

It is often said that in the moment prior to death, one's life flashes before them. One of the most frightening realizations someone can make is while looking back on their life, when face to face with death, and thinking," why didn't I?" or "I wish I..." Even the slightest doubt can set off a domino effect of regret. I live to prevent this from happening. I live to break rules, and to follow them. I live based on schedule, and I live spontaneously. I live for fun, and I live for work. I live for competition and I live for pleasure. I live in fear, and I live in bravery. I live for my future, and I live for this very moment here in front of me. And maybe even sometimes I will act to please others, but when the time comes and I am faced with death I will not regret, I will not doubt, I will have lived for me.

Each person on this planet is a unique, extraordinary human being with a set of beliefs, aspirations and a purpose in life. One is not made aware of their purpose, they must go in search of it or it is thrust upon them. One thing is for sure though; nobody's purpose is to live for someone else. Living for others and their approval is a crime. There should be a punishment for this crime; however it can be argued that one already exists – an unfulfilled life.

Mirrors are powerful things. At the end of the day, when you look in the mirror you have no choice but to face reality. One must look at the person staring back and come to the conclusion that they like what they see, or they don't. There is no in-between. This is where the power of a mirror comes into play. Reflection is technically just something in which shows the outward and physical appearance of things, but is this undoubtedly so? No. When looking in the mirror people see who they really are, inside and out. They face the decisions they have made, people they have hurt and even their accomplishments in life; this either pleases them or disgusts them. Disgust is what I live to prevent. Every single day of my life I wish to look in that mirror and be pleased with the person I have become.

It takes strength to do this and courage to live life to the fullest. Every person is given this strength and courage and has it somewhere hidden inside of them; some deeper than others. Some people need help to find it and some have these characteristics seeping through their pores. This is the reasoning why I believe so strongly in living for you. Because any reasoning why you can't is just an excuse — anyone can do anything and everything they please. It is only fear standing in their way, and fear cannot hurt anymore then a dream can. Aspiring to do this however, is rare. This is what separates those who are pleased with their reflection from those who are disgusted.

I hope to at least change one life for the better while I am here on this planet. I hope to pick someone up after they have fallen. I hope to give someone an opportunity they would have never have been exposed to. I hope to make people smile and I hope to fulfill my purpose on this planet to the greatest extent. I hope to love the person staring me back in the mirror. And one thing I know for sure is that I will not live with regret.

Just This

Just now

Just us

Just everything

Exactly how we are

Exactly what we were given

Just Love

Just Life

Just Hope

Exactly how it happens

Exactly the way we make it

Accept what and who you cannot change

Accept those who cannot do that

Accept redundancies and the unoriginal

Accept it and turn it in to something livable

Just for you

Just for us

Just for everything

Perfection is a myth

Hope is a virtue

Peace is a blessing

Love is a gift

Life is

Just life

Exactly how we live it

Just as we make it

Exactly what we choose

Accept and embrace all of it

Just because you deserve it

Knowledge of an In [between] Girl

To in-between people,

Welcome to the club. It isn't very glamorous, being that filler body, the warm and sympathetic soul who opens themselves to recently detached person. The commitment they put into their relationship with another person is what you often desired, or maybe you just want to jump their bones. Either way, we seek out these less than solid, emotionally off-kilter, people... Because for the life of us, we couldn't shake our attraction to them, even if they shook us off. Shook us away, but just close enough to call on when they needed reassurance that they are magnificent and fantastic.

We are those people. Are you not? We can have many names: rebound, tramp, ditz, piece of ass/muscle/dick, play thing, fuck friend, booty call, but my personal favorite is, "That person? Oh, they're just a friend, no one special." And those are what we can be called to our face. The list of other names are spoken in hushed whispers by friends of the detached individual, backstabbers, family, strangers, people sometimes you haven't spoken to in years.

See how the glamor fades, a bit? But take my word for it. Or maybe you should. See as a member, I know the benefits. Primarily: YOU ARE FINALLY WITH THEM. I mean, shit! How long have you been craving them? Weeks, months, years? Trust me, that initial shot of happiness only builds when they "finally see you were there all along". They saw you, but you weren't what they wanted, since you weren't tagged in the Facebook "X is in a relationship with NOT YOU". But that doesn't matter now, since they want you. Congrats, you can put down the Ben&Jerry's, but keep it nearby, you'll need it soon.

As the in-between filler, you have duties to fulfill. Nurse, comforter, friend, ally, the 3am call, and slowly work your body in there. Since you've been waiting a while for them, you can't WAIT to give yourself fully. Yowza! Break out the nice undergarments, bed sheets, and you are free to prowl! Just don't expect it to be totally fireworks. Whoever they split from had them too, and you might not be confident you're living up to them.

Know why? Nerves, excitement, and that deep-seeded need to perform, impress, and simply live up to the ghost of the past relationship. Kind of an unfair deal, ain't it?

These deals... they are no good. Look at yourself. You gave everything you had to be that NEXT GREAT MATE. But this isn't like a game show, you can't just win a spot as their next true love, if they, and quite frankly you, aren't ready for it. Great love isn't found in the bed of your beloved, as they sweat sex from their pores, and ask you if they should ask for their old CDs back from what's-their-face. The image of you finally connecting slowly bursts, shatters like a cleansing rain, as you are purified. Or some shit like that, just don't get too wrapped up in 90s female power music. But do reconnect with Ben&Jerry for a bit.

Not too long, but enough to realize everything dumb you just did. Because you are a great person, full of strong, pure, overwhelming love and you deserve to share it with someone who will give it back to you equally.

So... do you really want a membership? Because truthfully, I'm thinking about getting rid of mine.

To fellow LGBT teens...

I'm sure you spend every day being told what you are. Different. Weird. Confused... Infectious. Queer. Even some derogatory terms.

Do you have any idea how many LGBT youth end up committing suicide?

Statistically, you are more likely to commit suicide than to reach the age of 20.

And from what? Bullying.

I'm here to tell you something different.

I'm here to tell you what you aren't.

You are not weird.

You are not inhuman.

You are not infectious.

You are not unworthy of marriage.

You are not worthless.

You are not alone.

But most importantly, you are not a statistic.

Now, for what you are...

You are unique.

You are a gift.

You are talented, beautiful.

You are everything you could ever dream of being...

You do not need acceptance.

Not from school peers, teachers, parents or priests.

The only acceptance you need is your own.

Who cares what other people think.

Love yourself for who you are.

Stand up for what you believe in and don't let anyone tell you otherwise.

Those who mind never matter and those who matter never mind.

Please... Don't give up.

you are beautiful

To everyone who thinks they aren't, you are beautiful.

Don't ever let anyone tell you otherwise. No matter what you have been through, no matter how ugly you feel, just remember, you are unique, you are special, you have so much to contribute to this world, even if you don't know it.

To the girls who don't get the attention they want from boys, you are beautiful.

To the teenagers who feel unappreciated and smothered by their parents and teachers and coaches and everyone that ever sees them, you are beautiful.

To the girls who look in the mirror and wish they were thinner, you are beautiful.

To the kids who can't seem to get their skin to clear, you are beautiful.

To the girls who aren't as curvy as they would like to be, you are beautiful.

To the boys and girls who aren't prom king or queen, you are beautiful.

To the ones who sit on the computer making programs and doing other really brilliant things, you are beautiful.

To the misunderstood girl who works so hard to be popular, because she fears being alone, you are beautiful.

To the people who are teased, mocked, and otherwise tormented, either physically or emotionally, you are beautiful.

To the people who express themselves through art, and have a wonderful gift, you are beautiful.

To the individuals who are different, whether by choice or by nature, you are beautiful.

To every single person who was ever born, you are beautiful, you are important, you are special.

I know it sounds cheesy, but I don't think you are told this enough. You are worth every battle, you are worth every penny, you are worth every minute of time. You are rare, you are desired, you are wonderful. Don't ever let anyone make you feel otherwise.

For the bruised and the wounded;

My whole life I've been searching for the answers. The answers to what? I don't know. I just wanted to know. I wanted to know everything. I wanted to know what it felt like to love and not be hurt, or, really just how to prevent being hurt. I wanted to fix my broken heart, to mend my wounds, to heal my scars. I searched and searched and couldn't figure out how to fix myself.

How do you get over heartbreak? With the mindset that everything happens for a reason? Believing that if you were meant to be you would fall back into each other's arms? Believing that those who have died are in a better place, that they haven't completely gone, that they are still in your mind and your heart and everything around us. Yes, that can help- temporarily. For a brief moment you might feel relieved, feel hopeful again. For a second or two you might look outside and think:

"Hey, my life is pretty awesome; I should really suck it up and just live."

And sometimes those thoughts and feelings of joy last even longer; they make you think you've healed.

Until, one day, you come across a reminder of that event or that person that caused you so much pain, may it be driving into the sunset, hearing a song, a laugh, a joke. Reading a letter, this letter even, that sets off the feeling of being suffocated, of sinking and never wanting to come up for air. The memories come flooding back, overwhelming you with grief, with despair.

Alas once again you suck it up, you tell yourself to cut it out, you should be over this by now, right? Normal people heal fast, right? Maybe if you shove those thoughts deep deep down, they'll be far enough down that they won't resurface...right?

No. No. No. This is the point where you need to embrace these feelings. You need to scream, you need to cry, and yes, it is OKAY to talk about it. It's okay to sob your heart out until you feel like you're all dried up. It's okay to FEEL. You NEED to feel.

I know this sounds scary, terrifying even, why would you want to feel hurt, betrayed, cheated, abandoned all over again? You don't want to feel these feelings because whoever or whatever it was that hurt you was so heart wrenchingly painful, you can't bear to think about it.

Well let me tell ya, I've tried everything, I've had people leave, people die, and people rip my heart out without a second thought. I thought that I was supposed to be fine with it all, cry for a day, maybe. I thought it was better to not think about it. I thought that if I didn't think about it or talk about it that it would just go away. Instead it festered inside me until it resurfaced causing issues I didn't think could happen just by not thinking about something. I thought that I needed to be happy with my life because in so many ways it is so wonderful. But I realized that even if you have a wonderful life, it doesn't mean that this terrible thing didn't happen, it doesn't mean that if you take time to be sad about this thing that you are ungrateful for everything else.

What I'm trying to say is, it takes a long time to heal. To truly heal.

So screw all of those sayings about things getting better, screw all of your friends for telling you it's time to move on. They're not you. They don't know how much this affected you. But just remember no matter how heart broken and alone you feel, there are many many others suffering along with you. Just read this site- see all these people hurting? But that does not mean that that takes away from your hurt, because you had your heart broken too.

And you need to cry, and you need to heal, and you need to be sad and angry and hurt for a while. That is okay, you are okay, and screw whoever it was that broke your heart.

Cry, scream, and go eat some ice cream. And when you're ready, talk about it.

Do it.

Just do it.

No, not like Nike.

Do it.

Hold the door open for a stranger.

Sit with the outsider at lunch.

Invite someone new to come along somewhere.

Stop the bullying.

Accept everyone.

Love everyone.

Listen to everyone.

Acknowledge everyone.

Because if you do, they'll do the same.

To whoever is reading this...

Hello you,

Yes you, reading this off the screen. I wanted to let you know something. Something which I hope will make you think and make your day.

It isn't a secret as such, it's something I believe everyone should know and start to believe. I think you are beautiful, you have so much potential, you are gorgeous (don't let anyone make you think differently), someone, somewhere, just like you, is waiting for you. They will wait and wait until they find someone exactly like you and when you find them it will be the most amazing experience that will ever happen to you.

Start to think about the positives, not the negatives. I want you to do this right now. List 5 things you love about yourself, what makes you feel good about yourself, when you look in the mirror, ignore the negatives. You have so much to give, whether it's your personality, inner beauty.

I promise you, the people around you think you are a beautiful/gorgeous person. Every day, when you and these people (whether it family/friends/people you barely know) and you make them laugh or you laugh together, this is beauty.

I can't express how deeply distressed I am with the world, with myself, of how people get so wound up about their looks, what isn't right. I've started to grow up and realise less is more. Being perfect isn't everything. I like my flaws, they've taught me well, as have mistakes and mishaps, things that have made me have to grow up and realise you only live once.

YOU ONLY LIVE ONCE. Stop living in the past, LIVE FOR NOW. If you don't like your job, quit and find something that you love. If you look at yourself daily comparing yourself to other people, you will never get anywhere, you are beautiful, Mother Nature gave you this shabang for a reason. If you think you're too tall, embrace it, wear heels, show of those killer legs. If you're too short, hell girl, boys always think you're cute. If you don't like your face but you love your eyes or mouth, then learn to apply make-up (but not too much – LESS IS MORE) then get the mascara out. Natural beauty is the most beautiful thing one can find, so please, please use it.

Finally, YOU ARE A BEAUTIFUL AND AMAZING HUMAN BEING. THIS WORLD IS BEAUTIFUL. TAKE CHANCES. LIVE YOUR LIFE. NEVER LET ANYONE PUT YOU DOWN. DO SOMETHING WITH YOUR LIFE. LIVE AND LEARN TO LOVE AND APPRECIATE ALL THAT YOU HAVE AND THAT IS AROUND YOU.

finally, I will be forever yours, whoever you are, wherever you are.

From A x

Cheers to Us

This is for the guys like me. For the best friend, to the crying shoulder, the middle of the night call recipient- you know what I mean. This is for the guys who are so close yet so far. You watch her slip away, and then come back, and then you have a chance and then- bam. Nothing. This is for the guys who have wiped away the tears, made her laugh, just to see her smile. This is for the guys who write poem after poem or song after song, but never get the chance to perform it This is for the guys who sit and wonder "Why me?" This is for the guys who are stuck in the friend zone, but could imagine spending your entire life with her. You're the tutor, the best friend, the coach, the therapist- all beautiful things, but not the title you deserve. This for all those guys just like me- hoping, dropping hints, proving that chivalry isn't dead.

So here's to hope, gents. Here to hope that we'll no longer be the guy like that.

Live Your Life

Dear Whomever May Come Across This,

I don't know you, and you probably don't know me, but if you're feeling scared or upset or broken or hurt or lonely or lost or frustrated, I just want you to know that you are not alone. Life will bring challenges that can break us down and tear us apart, but were all in this together although it may not seem that way. When you're scared, face your fears and know that you are stronger than you think. When you're feeling lost, know that you will find your way. When you feel alone, know that you never are. When you feel tired and just want to give up, don't. Stand. Stand up and push past your limits. Stand up for your beliefs and never be ashamed of who you are. Always remember that behind every mistake, there is forgiveness. It is never ever too late to start over or try something new. Live your life passionately, deeply, meaningful, & truthfully. Tomorrow is always a new day, and when it comes choose to make it count because you'll never get it back. I don't know anything about you and you don't know anything about me either, but I know that you weren't put on this Earth by accident, and God has an amazing plan for you and for me and each one of us. I wish you a life full of happiness, love, and amazing days that you never want to end.

Love,
Someone who knows how fragile life is

a letter to humanity

Dear fellow human,

There are 7 billion of us. Think of all of those people, those souls. I bet some of them feel just as alone as you do.

We are so alike. All of us. All of us people with hopes and dreams. All of us with things we care about more than anything. Why do we set ourselves apart? Why do we keep people out of our lives? Why do we refuse to reach out? Why do we refuse to get along?

We are so different. All of us. All of us with our own unique ambition. All of us with our different religions, different pasts, different talents. Why do we sometimes feel as if we don't matter? You do matter, there is only one you. That's what makes us special.

You are special.

Everyone is here to complete a beautiful picture. We can't see it because we are looking at it too close. But if we take a step back, we can see the masterpiece. If pieces of the masterpiece decided to disappear it wouldn't work anymore.

You are part of something much bigger then yourself.

I think you have probably figured out by now that you don't have control of the universe. You don't always decide what happens to you. Sometimes things just suck. So stop blaming yourself. Your job is to turn things that are ugly into something beautiful.

Look at life with a smile. Become an optimist. See the best in everything, even when you feel like crying. Count your blessings. If you have eaten in the past day and have a roof over your head you are more fortune than almost half the world.

This is your life.

And life is short.

Savor each moment. Stop just to breathe in the air. Talk to someone you haven't talked to in a while. Go someplace new. Plant something just to watch it grow.

Enjoy every bite you take, love the friends you make, count the stars on those nights you stay awake.

Don't just wait around for someone or something to give you purpose. Waiting is for cowards. Go out there and make your own purpose. Be crazy, make people wonder, try new things, laugh through your tears, and have fun doing it.

<3

More

Dear Child,

You are loved. You are cherished. You are fully known and wholly, truly, deeply loved. There is Someone out there who thinks about you every moment of every day.

Some days life seems like it has no meaning, that the pain you suffer through is endless and meaningless. It is NOT! There is a plan for your life. These hard times you're going through are all part of what will make you the beautiful person you are going to become.

Your life has so much purpose! Whether it's to save someone's life through your career, a single action, or just a smile when they're having a bad day. Whether it's to change the course of history, or to simply make life worth living. Look for that purpose, find the meaning. I promise it's there.

And, please, please, please! Don't neglect yourself. Take time to enjoy the beauty of creation. Take time to bask in the presence of your friends and loved ones. Take time for yourself to recover, rejuvenate, recharge. Your life is intended to be abundant. Part of that IS struggles, but the other part is straight up joy and satisfaction and awesomeness!!

So, get enough sleep, take care of your body, do things you love, learn to love who you are, because I KNOW there is at least 2 people out here who you mean the WORLD to.

To everyone who is ever scared to do something in the name of love...

Man. Up. Seriously. I see so many posts on here by people who have let something slip away just because they were "too scared" to let something happen, or of what might happen, or of messing it up. Don't get me wrong, I do understand, but I've been at the receiving end of someone being too scared and letting what we had down and it hurts us too, and scares us even more when we finally move on to someone else.

If you want something, if it's right – ignore the fear and go for it. Just go for it. If you fall, so what? It happens to everyone, so pick yourself up and carry on, try again and again until something sticks if you have to. Just go for it!

xx

You Will Get Through This.

In August of last year, my boyfriend was killed in a car accident. We had been together for 5 months, but I felt like I had known him my whole life. I am 18 years old, and some of you may be thinking, "You're too young to know what love is" or "You weren't with him long enough to know if you were in love". But I can guarantee all of you that I was in love. Head over heels. The kind of love people dream about...I had it for a brief amount of time and then it was ripped out from under me.

These past 10 months have been some of the hardest months I have ever experienced. The loss of someone you love is unbearable. You want to fall down and never get up again. You feel as if you're world has been shattered, and there is no way to put it back together. You feel as if you'll never find a love like that again.

This letter is to anyone who has been through hard times. The times that you think you'll never make it out of. I'm here to tell you that you will get through this. You will make it out of the darkness, and back into the light. There are better times ahead. The sad times don't last. It does get better. Yes, it takes time, but I promise you, you will heal.

Don't let the darkness swallow you whole. Fight to become better. Fight to stay alive and see one more sunny day. Smile when you think you want to cry. Cry when you need to let out the sadness. Scream when you don't get answers you've been searching for, but don't stop searching for them. Laugh. I know sometimes you may think, "I shouldn't be laughing", but you're alive. You are still on this earth, living your life, so LAUGH. Be alive, even when all you want to be is dead.

You will get through this.

All you have to do is fight.

Fight to live a happy life.

You will make it through the tough times.

I promise.

I.Love.You.

For anyone wondering who this is written for, it's for whoever cares to read it.

I love you. I love you more than you can imagine. I love everything about you.

Please don't change. Please light up the world with your smile. Please laugh until you cry.

Dream until your dreams come true. Dream of the world with more people like you. Dream of all that you can be.

Reach for the Stars. Reach for your goals. Reach for something you never thought you could.

Dance like no one's watching. Dance in the rain. Dance until you can't feel your feet.

Jump up and down with joy. Jump over anything that tries to stop you. Jump into your nice cozy bed.

Forgive people who are mean. Forgive people who lie. Forgive people who want to bring you down.

If you can't beat them, beat them, so you have the element of surprise. If you are angry don't be cruel. If you are feeling down read this again.

Be smart. Be funny. Be kind. Be gentle. but most of all please please please just be YOU.

Always remember there are people who love you. If you are feeling like there aren't just know that I do. For most of you I have probably never met you, but know that you mean the world to me... and probably many others. Keep your head up and smile.

To Those In Secret Love

To whom it may concern,

To those in love, but are too afraid to do something about it,

It breaks my heart to read your letters about a male or female who is so amazing in your eyes, to read about all these feelings you keep bottled up inside. I understand the need to hide your feelings, but believe me when I say it's never worth it. SPILL YOUR SOUL. SHOW THE WORLD AND THE PEOPLE IN IT YOUR HEART. The worst case scenario is NEVER as bad as never trying, as never taking a risk. LEAP FORWARD. DIVE RIGHT IN. Life's too short to be afraid of heartache, to be afraid to lose someone you love. You can't lose someone if you never had them in the first place! "It is better to have loved and lost than to have never loved at all!"

Please, I'm begging this of you, of all of you. No matter what your circumstances, whether it be gender related, you're dating someone else, your parents disapprove, your friends don't like them, they live far away, you're afraid to lose a friendship, FORGET WHY FOR ONE SECOND, forget why you're afraid to love them and just LOVE THEM.

Tell the one you love them today, before it's too late.

Sincerely concerned,

MissNikkii

Be somebody

Be somebody.

Somebody right now.

Be the person who does something so wonderful that jaws drop.

Be the one who changes somebody's life in an instant.

Be the guy who proves there is such thing as a man who never strays.

Be the woman who shows people there is more to a girl then her body, there is a strong willful mind.

Be the miracle nobody believed in, till you proved them wrong.

You WILL Find It

Dear you,

Every single human being on this planet and beyond, every man and woman, are deserving of love in every way.

You, me, everyone. We deserve that best friend, that special someone.

No matter how fucked up we are. No matter how terrible a person we believe ourselves to be. No matter how hopeless life seems, and don't even say you don't deserve love because you're not attractive, because YOU ARE BEAUTIFUL, and love is there.

And that is why you will never be truly alone. That is why you WILL find someone.

Because you DESERVE it.

So keep searching, keep looking, there is someone out there for you, and you will find them.

Never lose hope.

A
LETTER
TO
SOMEONE SPECIAL

Everything will be alright

Thank you for introducing yourself into my life. I wish the circumstances were different so that I could have gotten to know you better and much earlier. In either case, I'm still happy for having met you and I know that distance is a killer when it comes to keeping in touch (for us anyway) but I hope to see you again soon and hopefully we'll have an easier time opening ourselves up to each other.

One day I hope you realize that talking about yourself to people will not always result in judgment calls and that the world is on your side. I would do the best of my ability to try and convince you of that, and maybe I will the next time we meet again.

Until then,

Sing your heart out and have no fear

You

Dear you,

You know who you are. I expect you will read this. Let me tell you about something. You are a generous, loving, beautiful woman. I love you with all of my heart. I see a pain and struggle inside of you that I know is wearing you thin. I want to be selfish and say that I need you here. I want to know how our story ends up. Good or bad. I love you so much it hurts sometimes. I feel helpless sometimes. I see the problems and I can't fix them. You are funny, sexy and my best friend. You write great poems! You worry about me. You accept me for who I really am. You are a great person. I see how you look at me and it makes me smile. You mean a lot to a lot of people. I know it's hard for you to see that sometimes but it's true. So I guess what I am saying is, I love you.

PS I am thinking about Ohio...

LOVE

ME

Love and Happiness

Closure, the word itself seeks definition. When is it over over...? I have been trying to define what closure means between us.

Is it when we say something in anger and never talk again? Is it when we ignore the past and move forward? Or is it when things simply fade away?

Closure for me, has been a dynamic. I can look back and remember all things said. All things unsaid. The memories really paint a pretty wide rainbow of emotions, ideas and feelings.

But really, I think I have arrived.

I am finally at peace. I have searched and searched for reasons. While all are debatable those that are not are my own actions.

I realize now through much personal deliberation and many painfully slow changing ideas where I stand in all of this. Put simply, what I did wrong.

I think back and see all the clear signs how I slowly pushed you away. I didn't take pleasure in the little details, chances to express my love. Simple things, like bringing you flowers, greeting you with a smile when you got home from business trip, going out with you to all the places I didn't care to go, not because I wanted to, but because YOU wanted to. So many things I can remember doing wrong, so many little things....so funny that there isn't anything bigger in the end.

It is clear to me reflecting on all the things you bought me, some only nick-knacks really, but an ever present reminder of the love you showed me. Each cute little stuffed animal reminding me of the way you would smile, each piece of paper I find with the words "I love arf" written everywhere a blank spot was.....so many places it seems like everywhere I look a piece of you is there.

I can see how I didn't express the love I hold for you. While I never spoke hollow words when telling you I Love you. I failed miserably at demonstrating the way I felt through day to day action. So, through the years we went, my selfish lifestyle and attitude slowly whittled away at your patience and love. Alas, and the way I tried to control you....seemingly so inconsiderately and overbearing... I didn't know how to let go and let you be you. I was wrong. The only right thing to do when you love something is to set it free. Yet another area I failed you.

I have to say reflecting on all of this has given me a profound amount of respect for how you held on. Against everything I didn't do, all my failures as a boyfriend, you stood by me, patiently waiting for me to wake up. In the end it took losing you and almost a year of reflection for me to see how special you really are.

I'd say thank you a million times if it conveyed any of what I really mean to say. As it stands the words thank you don't come close to describing the way I feel. 'Happy' and 'Appreciative' seem to belittle the way I feel about having been a part of your life.

I am so very proud you made the right choice. You have helped me grow in ways that are inexplicable by words. I entered the relationship a boy, and left a boy, now I feel as if I am finally on my way to being a man. I have hope, I have confidence, and I have learned a great deal about how to treat a REAL woman.

It is humbling that I was given the chance to be with someone like you. I can see clearly now how far I had to come, how far I still have to go, and have a much better idea of who I am.

I don't intend to send this letter, but thought it might be a good healing exercise to write it.

My hope is that you are at peace and with it, new life, love and happiness.

Before I say goodbye I would like to say:

I love you.

May you live to love and love to live.

Daniel

Don't ever.

Don't ever tell me that you hate yourself. You have no idea how many people love you just the way you are. Your imperfections make you perfectly human, and make me love you even more. Every time you look into a mirror, try and see yourself the way you see me... then maybe you will understand. You are perfect, no matter what, that will never change. I've never seen a future with anyone until you. I will always be there to hold you together when you feel like falling apart, just let me see what's in your heart.

You're not pathetic.

You're beautiful, you really are. I don't understand how you can see yourself as pathetic. You're talented and kind. You put up with my craziness. You can write lyrics; no matter how much you say you can't, you can. You have this poetic way of speaking that captivates me. Sometimes you make me want to cry because you can't see how amazing you truly are. Stop looking down on yourself. Stop holding on to your past. So what if you're a little bit messed up? Name one person who isn't. Who cares if most people repulse you? Most people repulse me too. I just wish I could help you and fix you. So what if she doesn't want you back? I want you. I love you. I wish you could see that, that's the only thing I'll ever truly wish for.

I Want To Wish...

If I could only tell you what I'm feeling... because I want to wish you the world.

I want to send you the moon and stars in small enough space to carry in your pocket. So when your beautiful smile leaves your face, the light of the night time sky can light it up again.

You are my soul mate, my other half, and I only wish I could tell you.

I wish you happiness, that someday you will find someone who will treat you how you should be treated, and how I would treat you.

If only I could have you... but I can't...

I want to wish I could be yours...

Wish Right Now

You're far better than you know.

Far, far better.

You're one of the nicest guys I know, and you deserve more than you think you do. I'm almost positive that half the people you meet fall in love with you in one way or another, and the other half wish they could know you better.

It's too strange for me to tell you all these things, because of how great of friends we are. You would never take it the wrong way because of how little you think of yourself, yet I feel that telling you would be too...telling, to coin a phrase.

One day you'll realize that the people who are the unlucky ones are the ones that no longer are in contact with you, not the other way around. Anyone with half a brain would make sure they keep you as a friend for as long as they possibly can. After all, you're going to be famous someday.

At some point, you'll find that lucky girl who will show you how absolutely great you are and I hope for your sake that it is a lot sooner than it is later.

I'm glad that I found you, someone where the friend zone feels comfortable on both sides. Yet, you need not worry that it will be that way for all. For you, the perfect gentleman who is not a gentleman at all.

You're one of those people worth keeping, and you don't need to change a thing.

Keep following those shooting stars; it is not as far as you think.

Chubby Guys

Dear Chubby Guys of the world,

Do not change. You are some of the sexiest people I have ever seen in my life! I am a diehard chubby chaser, and I really need some eye candy haha.

In all seriousness though, I really do find that chubby guys are some of the best guys out there! They are nice, funny, and great at cuddling. I would prefer cuddling to a chubby guy over a bony one any day!

I hope to marry a guy that will forever be my chubby lover. So if you are out there, reading this, look for me because I am looking for you!

Love

You:

I just wanted to tell you how special you are.

Maybe people see that, and maybe they don't; but I do. You are so nice. And you care. You're just a genuinely nice person. I admire that. I love that.

I think we belong together.

It may not seem that way to you, but it does to me. And I just know it's supposed to be. I only wish you could see that. I could make you happy...er. You are perfect for me, and I for you. I just hope that, one day, you'll feel the same way. But for now, I'm just glad that you're a friend of mine.

That's all.

Sitting forlorn on the Sidewalk

Are you okay?

I ask because I know I heard and saw you sitting there crying to yourself. Your state of mind didn't matter, maybe you could only show your raw feelings when you think you're alone.

Sometimes I'll ask you what's wrong, you'll say "Nothing, thank you" And you move along, embarrassed that some stranger noticed.

Sometimes I'll say nothing, leaving you to yourself, hating myself for not being able to help.

I'm sorry for what happened. I'd give you a hug, but don't know if you want that.

Please feel better, remember that even strangers care. Remember you don't have to always be the strongest.

Try to smile, if only out of amusement at the situation, it'll go a long way.

oh, I'll never let you fall.

Even when I yell and scream and curse, even when I have a mood swing, even when I'm not in the mood to cuddle, even when I seem distant.

I will always be here for you, even if I can't always say it, even if I have trouble proving it.

I know it, you know it. I love you. I worship you, actually, because you are such a good person. You are almost perfect, if there was such a thing.

Hello the rest of my life, you are dear. I will be the one you can turn to, you can cry to me, on me, yell at me, hurt me, because I can take it all on for you, just to see you smile again, I want you happy completely forever.

I want to be for you, what you are for me, my lover, my best friend, my savior in ways, my sounding board when I'm upset, my playmate. You are so much to me.

Tell me what to do, you got it.

Just know...

that I am thinking of you and holding you close to my heart. You are a great person and I want what's best for you. I know what and who you seek in your heart. I am trying to help you stay true to your values and mine.

It's not easy and I'm not sure what the answer is of yet.

I know it is not what either of us wants to hear but we must walk in the spirit and not in the flesh.

Relax. Find Peace and have a nice day. Try to...for me:)

To My Love

You are the best thing that has ever happened to me. You are my best friend, my confidant, and my lover. You've cried on my shoulder, and I on yours. You tell me you want me to be the mother of your children, and that you want me to marry you when the time is right. You gave me my first kiss ever a few nights ago. I am so unconfident that I thought I would never be worthy of love, and felt so ugly that I thought I would never be kissed. But you kiss me every night, every day, and you never forget to tell me you love me. And you're hurting now. I know you're putting on a front for me, but the grief for your loss is there underneath, even six months later. It's okay. You don't have to fake it for me. I want and love you in whatever state of damaged goods you come in. I wish that I could take away your grief, take it on myself so that you don't hurt, but that isn't possible. I am not God, and that is hard for me to accept. But I will be here for you, as you have always been for me. I love you. And you'll get through this. And I'll be here.

Who God Wants Girls To Be With

When my hero of a father passed away...

You held me close
Soaked in my tears
Whispered Softly
"I'll take care of you now"
Then
You told me not to turn to you
But to turn to God
This is why I love you. And you are the type of guy that heavenly and earthly fathers want me to be with.

Thanks

Mom

Dear Mom,

I just want you to know how much I love you. How lucky we are to have such an amazing mother like you. What would I do without you? Not only did you bring me into this world but you love me more than anything else in the world, you gave up everything for me, e v e r y t h i n g. I'm sorry I have been so ungrateful and horrible at times. I was angry growing up, but as the years have passed I've realized just how selfish and petty I was. I am so thankful for everything in my life even though at times I feel as if the world is on my shoulders and I have no idea how to carry it for one more day, but then I think of you. With 3 small children left alone in a big empty house while dad was away when he should have been at home taking care of us. How strong you are, you are so beautiful inside and out. I love you mom and I hope one day I can be half of the woman you are. I just want to give you everything in the world, because you deserve so much more. Even though we didn't get along for most of my adolescence I am truly sorry. I would take a bullet for you, I love you and I owe you my world.

With all my love,

Your daughter

bravery

Dear Woman in line in front of me at the tattoo parlor,

Good for you! You got your navel pierced in front of strangers. You told the piercer, "Yes, those are my C-section scars." You said you were doing this for YOU.

My friend made fun of you, but I told her to shut up.

You're beautiful.

Time to Grow Up

I know how scared you are. Scared of failing, scared that everything you've done up to this point was a mistake. You're scared that you will have no idea how to handle yourself "in the real world". The responsibility is a huge one, yes, but it's one that you will continually grow into. If this is what you want, you will do it, and you'll do great at it. The next few months will be very stressful, emotional, and difficult, and they will test you, but they will make you stronger. Before you know it this time in your life will be over. Soon you'll be graduating and getting a job, moving out to God only knows where. This is your chance to prove to yourself that you can live up to your own expectations. You can take responsibility for yourself and take steps to move your life forward. It's time for you to start taking care of your own life; you're not a little kid anymore.

My Sparrow

My Sparrow,

Fly on love. Fly on and take these winds against your face as a gentle kiss from what's to come. Fly on love. Fly on and take the tempests by storm. Try as they might, they will not stop you. Don't you dare let them stop you. Fly on love. Fly on through the barriers that they whispered you couldn't break. Break them. Break them all.

Don't forget me my sparrow, when you've reached your home in this life... When you reach the place where you can rest your tired wings. Don't forget me my sparrow, when you gaze upon the universe for what you've made it to be.

Condor Ave

To any girl that has ever look at me and smiled,

First off, thank you for making my heart melt in a complete way right into my chest. I don't know why i want to give my heart away to every girl with striking eyes and a true smile you only know when you see it. I find happiness in those moments when you were just purely perfect to me, those seconds replay in my mind all day every day. I want to give my heart to you so badly only if i could find the right one to make it all possible. I can only do a couple things good in life. I want to draw you pictures, pictures of the things you love. I want to make you feel as if you were the most incredible person on the planet. The other night at that indie party it happened again. Katie, you have the most epic smile eyes combination i have seen. I felt... I actually felt it was nice to think about how badly i wanted to make you fall in love with me at that moment. I feel your already fading away from my thoughts. I look at your pictures on facebook in hopes of getting back to the moment in which you were perfect to me, so pure and real. I love so hard and it sucks. I want you to love me so badly. I want to make you smile uncontrollably when you think of me. I never want the thought of me to leave your mind. I want to make you smile. I really want to make you smile. Let me do the nicest things in that my mind could ever come up with for you. I love falling for whoever you are. So don't ever smile at me again if you don't want me make laugh like nothing else in the world matter. All i did just now here is written exactly how i felt about you, funny thing is, I was with you for maybe an hour. -Tyler D.

It's The Last Thing I'd Say

If there is one thing that I've learned in this week, it's that today could be the last. And I realized that the terms I leave on would be that of regret. I'd regret not telling you I care more than you'd ever know that you are my world and my rock. I've never learned how to be respected by a man until I met you. Having you in my life has changed who I am, how I go about my life, and how I love. You have been perfect and I know sometimes I can be rude, but it's because I want you to express that you care through your words. You show me through your actions every day, but knowing that I matter and that you want this to last is what I want. Life is too short for me sit here and wait for an answer, oh how I'd wish you'd tell me these things. Because the last thing I'd Say if it ended today would be you are and always will be the one who breathed life into my sinking body. I need you always.

It's love.

I want to spend my life with you. I want to be with you, be yours, marry you, be in your life forever.

I want to grow old with you, raise our kids together, cuddle every night, tell each other about our days and share our dreams.

I want to be one of those cute old couples our grandkids can look up to to see what "love" truly is.

More than anything, I want you to know that you are the world to me. I love you more than I ever thought possible. You changed my life – maybe you even saved my life.

I won't love you until the day you die; I'll love you until the day I do.

We were meant for each other, let's prove it. If forever is all we have, I want to start right now. I love you.

You did so much more...

Growing up I went to church. My mom was never really religious but my grandpa was. We went to church every Sunday. I always had the best attendance. I grew up in that church. When I was old enough I went to church camps and I tried out to be a Central Area Officer. I made it and it was the scariest thing I ever did. I was so proud of myself, though.

Well, sh*t happens. Slowly, I didn't even realize it, I started losing my faith in not only God but in the goodness of people. I've always felt a bit empty inside.

Last week, the town I live in got a snow storm and school was let out. A couple days into this impromptu break I felt the need to go to this barn out in the country I've loved since I moved here at seven. I knew it was stupid, the roads were slick with ice and since I was going into the country I knew there would still be snow piled all over the roads. I have a small car, as well, a Nissan Maxima.

Well, I made it to the barn just fine then I was too nervous to try and back out and turn around for fear of getting in the ditch. So I was driving and I took this turn that I knew would lead me to my road. Halfway to the end though I get stuck. My first thought was: "Gee, awesome!" Luckily, I was hundred feet away from this little, slightly creepy house. I called my mom to tell her I was going to this house to ask for some help and if I went missing at least she knew where I last was.

I knocked on the door and this sweet older woman answered. I explained my issue and she invited me in her house. She helped her husband get his boots and cap. They were the sweetest couple I've ever met. I apologized a thousand times for interrupting their life. They laughed it off. Her husband went to his truck and I walked back to my car. He hooked up his rope to my car and pulled my car out. He was so sweet about it.

Unfortunately, I don't remember their names. To them, they just pulled out my car of some snow and sent me on my way. But, to me, they restored so much of what I lost. They restored my faith in the goodness of people. And, even more importantly, I suppose, my faith in God. I've yet to go to my church yet because this all seems too shaky. I'm so scared to go back to that time when I believed in nothing.

Basically, I just wanted to say thank you so freaking much for everything you didn't know you did. I wish I could repay you for everything you did.

Iris, this is for you...

You are strong. Regardless of how weak you feel the moment those enchanting eyes open and you turn over to hit your alarm. Regardless of how you feel when you hear his voice or hear his name even though the name isn't a reference to him specifically. Regardless of how exhausted you feel when you finally slowdown from being the warrior I know you are.... Because you are a warrior. A fighter. An Adonis that lights up the world around herself until the universe just wants to be in the same room as you. Whose smile illuminates the very same mask you put on every day. But like I said, I see the mask, but I'd also never ask you to take it off. I'm also the one who sees right through it.... still. Though that mask has changed over the 5 years, it is still a mask... and I still see through its pellucid state... it's transparent, filminess and I see the mercenary underneath. Oh the wonders you've conquered! The miracles you've created and seized with just a gentle nod of your head and the shrug of your shoulders... though even I know that in front of every warrior is a shield. You are strong. Regardless of how often that blade fails you and eventually it falls to the tiled bathroom floor. Regardless of how defeated you feel when the tears have all fallen and the feelings are done bleeding from your soul. But oh blessing, you are the war that wages on through the years, the power beneath my blade and the sincerity in my heart. But oh confident, you are the swiftness of my feet and the sway of my words. But oh godsend, you are the vigor of my spirit. And I am strong because you are strong. <3

Listen

Dear,

First of all, I love you. You are the greatest influence that my life has ever had. You are the person who raised me, loved me, picked me up, taught me, remembered me...and who told me to be strong.

I am forever gracious.

But out of everything you have done for me, I know you have suffered. I know that sometimes you have dreams that hurt you so bad you ache, and you cut yourself off from me. You wish for death.

But why? You are my sunshine? You are the reason I grew up happy, instead of in a gutter. You are my atmosphere.

Why haven't you noticed that God made you for a purpose?

Better yet.

Why haven't you realized that you are MY purpose?

I love you. Nothing is worth leaving the party early, especially when the party is life.

smile

B.

There isn't one day i go without thinking about you. Wondering what you are doing while I am smiling, hoping you are doing the same. I honestly gave you everything I had and tried to make you realize the kind of amazing person you should know you are. It hurts you know, when the person you trust the most, let in to know you the most, completely change. Into some sort of stranger living in the next room. You are beautiful. You are worth it, and you do not deserve to be sad. You do need to wake up one day and realize that your sorrow puts everyone around you on edge. You need to wake up and take responsibility of your life and hold it by the reins and live. Live with no fear, and don't be bothered with what people think. I will always miss who you were and what you meant to me. I will not forget who you became, and I will never forget how you hurt me.

Just smile, life isn't about being the leading lady you see in the movies. It's about making the most out of every moment you can.

A.

Think of Me.

This is for you.

Think of me. Of our yesterday's happiness. Bitterness gone. To be bitter is to forget. To ruin what we had. I am not bitter. We loved. We lost. It's simple. I choose to be happy. Choose the same.

Think of me. I'll think of you. We will never lose each other, just be separated by time. And that's okay. Everything will be okay. I promise. You promised.

Think of me. Imperfect. The good. The bad. How I was. How we were. Then, let me go. Let me be a memory. You are a memory.

Think of me. On a beautiful day. Wish I am there. I will be. Together again in a memory. Untainted. Perfection. Forever.

Think of me.

Please

Please don't forget you mean the world to me. That you, yes you, are the reason I can still smile sometimes, when the world doesn't really give me much to smile about. Then you walk in the door and something enters with you. Some intangible feeling of warmth and heart. I now life is hard sometimes and I can see the downtrodden-ness in your eyes, in your smile. I can tell that you feel alone. You're not though, you never will because if nothing else, my mind is always with you. Please don't give up. You really are one of a kind and I don't think the world would have quite as much peace or the sun give off quite as much light if you didn't believe it too. For me, you're the center of the universe and I don't think you realize just how much life is in you. The whole world exists in your head and you can paint it any color you choose. The sky is blue because you believe it to be. Hell, the world turns for you. Now go out and start creating magic. Start seeing the joy in the world and the world will be joyful. It's all up to you.

A Friend Without Hope

I get it. You haven't exactly had the greatest life. Your mom was bipolar and drove you nuts. Your dad was a lunatic that was never there. You felt like a bitch when your mom died because you didn't think you were ever nice enough to her. I understand you better than you think.

This person you have been pretending to be for the past 3 years is not you. I know you think you've finally found yourself but i have never seen such a confused, scared shitless little girl in my life.

Quit making excuses for yourself. You do drugs to escape not for the 'experience'. You want out of this city because you think running away is the only way to escape yourself. But the truth is you're going to have to own up to life sooner or later.

I just hope it's before you make a mistake and ruin your chances in life. You are so incredibly talented, why are you throwing that away? Do you have any idea how thrilled i would have been to have a talent like yours that has turned into a passion? One that you can turn into a job?

I know you won't let anyone else help you; you've always tried to prove your independence. So show us your strength that you profess to have. Prove it.

this one's for the girl...

so here's how it is...
it's gonna be difficult.
and there will be tears.
and we'll get mad.
and we'll ask why.
and we'll fight it with everything we have.
but in the end... we'll get through.
we'll let go.
we'll feel whole again.
we'll feel happy again.
we'll FEEL again.
and then one day we'll be chosen.
we'll be put first.
we'll be treated how we should be treated.
and they'll wake up.
open their eyes and realize...
realize their mistake.
realize that the choice they made was wrong.
that we were worth the fight.
and now it's their loss.
they were our first.
they were our best friend.
they were our world.
and even though we hate to admit it...
they made us who we are.
so i don't know why things happen this way.
i don't know why we get hurt... over... and over again.
all i know is that one day...
one day it'll be worth it.
i'm holding on to that promise.

Dear Mister Guy Next Door,

Hello,

I am writing you this letter as a form of encouragement. You, my suite mate and I are all good friends and as a good friend, I think I should be there for you no matter what. I know that loving someone is hard but you may never know how my suite mate feels about you until you tell her. It feels so much better when you do, trust me.

The way things are going now, it could only turn for worse. The more you hide your feelings, the more I notice you seem more lonely. You tried to hint to her your feelings, tried letting her know through touch, and even tried (in a very roundabout way and inputting me into it) asking her on a date. It didn't work because she is the type of person who needs it said straight forward. I've tried setting up openings for you, but you either fail to see them until too late or make some kind of joke that backfires.

Don't be frustrated and keep your chin up. You're a great guy and even if things don't work out, at least things can only get better. I love both of you like family, and I don't want you or her unhappy. Also know, that even if she does seem to show favoritism towards me, it's only because we are similar and so we bonded faster. No need to be jealous or upset. Just think of it as having a woman on the inside. If love is a battlefield, then I'm the spy (except I want a win win).

Of course, telling her or not is your choice and either way I'll root for you.

Best wishes,

Rufus Chicka

A Difference

You know, I don't have any idea who you are. Your name, your friends, nothing. All I know is that you were a senior at my school last year. And I'm willing to bet you know even less about me then I do about you.

You will never know what a difference you made. That day? I had gotten in a huge fight with my dad. He kicked me and he knocked me over. I was still shaking when you saw me, 3 hours later.

Thank you so much for stopping to tell a freshman that you didn't know to smile and that things would be okay. It honestly made a world of difference to me.

I want.

I've never wanted to see you hurt, I want so much for you to be happy, this is how I feel and, i hope one day it will make sense to you:

There are certain things you can't deny and, happiness falls into that category. You could spend each and every day trying to find happiness in the same place. Digging and searching deeper and deeper but, there is only so much labor one can withstand. It hits you one morning when the sun's rays kiss your face and your eyelids barely open, the thoughts pour in every opening of your body: you'll never find what you're searching for here. It takes just one small thought to worm its way into your brain and, the beginning of the end has arrived. I shouldn't describe this process like some disgusting parasite; instead the gift of a new life or a newly planted seed, yes that would be more fitting. It feels as though it may be a parasite though as you try to deny these thoughts from consuming you, to convince yourself that everything you're feeling is just a wave of being content. How long do you spend propping someone up, helping them not fall? How long do you spend aimlessly digging for buried treasure that's located half way around the planet? There is not one bone in my body that wants you to feel the pain that has ever too often been my familiar friend. My intentions are pure. The correct question is, how much am I willing to sacrifice? Am I supposed to spend the rest of my days sitting like a crutch cradling you from hurt? If I spread my wings tonight and fly away I promise you'll learn to stand on your two feet, it will just take time...

just thinking of you...

hey...

The past couple of days have been rough...i know. You just have to stick through it and stay strong.

Don't say you want to take your life...it killed me when you said that. I'm just glad i talked you out of it...I know it sounds pathetic, but afterwards, when we were off of the phone, just the thought...the thought of you not being around anymore...would get me teary eyed.

You're the girl i want to be with, you're the girl i need in my life....you're the girl i love. I know i won't ever stop loving you. NEVER. So don't ever say you want to kill yourself. Don't.

I want to grow old and grey with you...just remember that.

Keep fighting. The day will come when i will come and steal you away and never give you back. You're a tough, beautiful, amazing person.

I Love You.

Remember it. Please...

Hopeful dreamer

Oh, Eryn.

Stop thinking you're ugly or fat. Stop thinking you're not enough.

You're more than enough and you are beautiful, inside and out.

Believe in yourself. Everyone's already trying to bring you down, don't do their job for them.

Find out what it is you want, and go after it. Work for it, and work hard. You've got the potential to make a difference and everyone knows. Use it. I know you've got it in you; you have all the tools you'll ever need.

Stop thinking and overanalyzing; take action. Take a chance and prove it to everyone. Prove it to yourself. You could be the greatest, but you'll never know if you don't take a chance. Stop worrying that you'll fail and give it a shot. You're far more than you think you are.

If I could breathe into you courage and confidence and strength, you know I'd do it in a heartbeat. You're so beautiful that it hurts. I want you to know that you're wonderful and I wish I was the one for you. But as it is, I'm not, and you're meant for something greater.

The only thing holding you back...is you. I love you.

My Friend

Hey My Friend,

I know you. I know your soul. I see it in your eyes.

I long to give you what you need, even if it was for only a moment. You are so precious. So beautiful. So sweet, kind, loving...

I only wish others saw you the way I see you. I only wish that you could understand that you are absolutely amazing. And I never ever want you to think even once about changing who you are. You hear me? Never.

Your smile is full of lost joy. Your eyes scream for love. I want to give it to you. I really do.

Please know that whatever happens in life, that there is a purpose for you. You are here for a reason. Your family may be crap; your home may be dumpy. You may have no friends and you may fail all your classes. But I am begging you, PLEASE do not give up.

Because you are MY friend, and I love you.

Sincerely,
Hannah

You're Not Supposed to Live in the Past.

But it's necessary to look back on it sometimes, to remind you of who you shouldn't have been, who you never should be again.

That's why I'm writing you this letter. You're me, but six months younger. You're me, but stuck in a winter you're terrified you'll never get out of. You've never been so old and so young at the same time. I can see it in your face – you're really just a scared little girl, hugging a razor instead of a teddy bear. Baby girl, I wish you'd realize that the momentary comfort you draw from the sight of your blood is only an illusion. The high that the adrenaline brings will slowly fade out to just another low – a fact you're well acquainted with by now, which is why I'm begging you. Cry into someone's shoulder. Scream at the sky. Make snow angels in ten degree weather. Let emotion back into your life, experience natural highs and lows, and feel something other than numb.

I don't know if you need help. I never got it, and I'm still alive. I haven't cut since December. I'm no longer afraid that I have depression. But I do have those days – those weeks, really – where all I want is to slice up my skin again, where I'm convinced – just like you are – that I'd be better off dead. And maybe if I'd gotten help back when I was you, those weeks would never happen, or at least be few and far in between. But maybe not. It's up to you, baby girl. You're going to make it no matter what. I have faith in you, even if you've lost all faith in yourself.

You'll get through. Just remember that. The winter isn't endless, and the darkness doesn't last forever. Your black-and-white world can develop color again, if you let it. You just have to open up and stop hiding behind your skin. Let go of your fears and insecurities. No one is perfect, and, regardless of what you think, you don't have to be. Embrace who you are and accept it, because that's where your overwhelming sadness ends and the rest of your life begins.

It's a hard road, there's no denying it. But you can do it. There is hidden strength in you that you have forgotten about. You have the power to stop merely getting through life and start living it. It only takes one person: you.

Baby girl, please don't take yourself so seriously. Life shouldn't be endured; it should be celebrated. Find refuge in your friends and family. I know that you think no one cares, but you'd be surprised at just how many people do.

Don't give up. Winters don't have to be forever.

Learn to love yourself, and then there will be spring.

please cheer up!

Hello you,

It's me, again! I want you to know that i understand how difficult everything is for you at the moment. And i NEED you to understand that it is your responsibility to do something to change it.

Your coursework is stressing you out: get on with it, stop lying around worrying and actually sit down and do it you feel better once it out of the way.

Stop worrying that you have chosen the wrong boy! You know he makes you happy, he made you happy before the other one was in your life and you can live with him for now, if in the future he does prove to be the wrong one, well you know perfectly well that all things happen for a reason and that there is a good chance of another chance!

Your course is what you want you want to do, what you have always wanted to do and will be the making of you, its hard, its gets you down but like the medicine that works the best the taste is bad but the result is what you need.

Enjoying working this hard you will never need to do it again and you can learn so many skills to help you cope with the future.

You don't want kids, i know that you have only just realized this and i know that it is upsetting a lot of people but this is your decision and ultimately it is an easy to decision to change at any given time you can backtrack and say well maybe i am ready now. But don't let him push you or force your hand if you don't want kids till after your 30 then that's up to you. Ignoring your baby headed friends as much as they say you can't understand because you don't have kids there are plenty of things that they don't understand because they do have kids. Your life is not less valid because of this decision.

You are not now nor have you ever been fat. I know the silly diet you are on helps you to feel in control, and yes you do look better for losing a little weight but that is not a reason to be so critical of your appearance you are beautiful and really you know it, people aren't looking at you because you look strange but because you look so good please try to be happy with your appearance.

And finally practice what you preach, you are constantly helping people to see things from a more positive perspective, deep down that is still how you see the world and you just need to embrace it make that stupid voice shut up and listen to yourself properly.

I love you

love,
Youxxx

LISTEN UP

Your life is ahead of you. Just because you don't have something now doesn't mean you won't ever have it. You need to earn more, work harder life isn't easy and you can't get everything handed to you. When it comes to school don't give up just work harder when an obstacle is in your way. Get the tutor, stop being pathetic, and feel sorry about yourself because you just aren't smart enough to do it. YOU ARE! That brain can hold a crap load and you need to figure out how to work it. When it comes to love and relationships, be yourself, you have to stop being what you're not. Show who you are; don't be afraid or shy or else people will take advantage of you! YES they will and you always feel like shit after that happens, you need someone that really loves you, and that you are afraid to love to, but stop being afraid. You may get hurt, but that's what a good cry is for and some home loving. Please stop with the negatives that have been holding you back these past 4 years, where is the Carmen that didn't have a care in the world, the one that could make a crowd laugh, that can be herself and people will love her for it. They all miss her, and she's finally coming back, don't you dare ever lose her again, you are one of a kind and you are stronger than ever now. Stick with it dear and prove to yourself you can do it. ONLY YOU.

INDEX